THE GOSPEL FOR
AN AGE OF DOUBT

THE GOSPEL FOR
AN AGE OF DOUBT

BY

HENRY VAN DYKE

D.D. (PRINCETON, HARVARD, YALE), LL.D. (UNION)
PASTOR OF THE BRICK CHURCH IN NEW YORK

SIXTH EDITION REVISED
WITH A NEW PREFACE

" But if any speak not concerning Jesus Christ,
I look upon them as tombstones and sepulchres
of the dead, on which are written only the
names of men."
St. Ignatius, Epist. ad Phil.

NEW YORK
GROSSET & DUNLAP
PUBLISHERS

251 P
V 288
1896
Spring

cop. 2

Norwood Press
J. S. Cushing & Co. — Berwick & Smith
Norwood Mass. U.S.A.

PREFACE

Two years have passed since this book was first printed. A new edition is now prepared for popular use by leaving out the appendix and making the volume smaller.

In writing a new preface, I am glad of the opportunity to express my sincere gratitude to the many friends who have given the book a welcome in different parts of the world, and have translated its message into other languages. I wish to acknowledge also the benefit received from those intelligent critics who have pointed out some of its faults and shortcomings, and to make some brief reply to those other critics who have misconceived its purpose and misrepresented its meaning. But most of all I would like to say a word to make the spirit and aim of the book more clear, and so to bring it into touch with the personal life of those into whose hands it may fall.

It was written in the form of a course of lectures on preaching, on the " Lyman Beecher

Foundation," and delivered before the divinity students of Yale University. But the aim of these lectures was not to teach the art of making sermons. It was to accentuate the truth that the question, What to preach, comes first, and the question, How to preach, comes afterwards. A man must have a distinct message, clear and luminous to his own soul, — a message which comes to him with a joyful sense of newness and demands utterance, — he must feel the living fitness of this precise message to the needs of the world, before he can learn to deliver it with freedom and power.

The study of theology as a science is a very important study. The training of men in the art of preaching is a very valuable discipline. But the vital experience of faith is deeper and broader than the theories of theology. The art of preaching is worth little unless it serves to enrich and ennoble the larger art of living. Religion is the secret of this larger art of living. And the power of religion to inspire and guide men to purer, stronger, happier, more beautiful lives, does not depend upon the modes and forms in which it is preached, but simply upon the concrete gospel, the good news about God and the world, which it brings into their hearts.

The audience in the Yale chapel appealed to me less as students of theology, than as young men with a life to live and a work to do in the modern world, in the present age. Around them I felt the pressure of those great, mysterious forces which are silently changing the current of human thought and the face of human society. Behind them I saw the wider circle of the young men and women of the new generation, the children of this age, born into the turmoil and confusion, the intellectual stress and storm, of a period of transition. It was to this wider circle that I really wanted to speak, through the divinity students who composed the immediate audience. I wanted to tell the men who were studying for the ministry that they must not let themselves be educated out of sympathy with the modern world; that they must understand the trials and difficulties of the present age in order to serve it effectively; that they must keep in touch with living men and women, outside of the circle of faith as well as within it, if they wished to help them.

But more than this. I wanted to show that there is a message of religion especially fitted to meet the needs of our times. There is an aspect of Christianity which comes to the world to-day as glad tidings. There is a newness in the old gospel which shines out like a sunrise upon the darkness and despondency that over-shadow so much of modern life. This aspect of Christianity centres in the person of Jesus Christ, as the human life of God. This new-ness of the gospel lies in believing in Him as a real man, in whose sonship the Fatherhood of God is revealed and made certain to all men. And the power of this message to enrich and ennoble life lies in the fact that those who receive it are set free from a threefold bond-age : first, from the heavy thought that they are creatures of necessity whose actions and destiny are determined by heredity and en-vironment; second, from the haunting fear that the world is governed by blind chance or brute force ; and third, from the curse of sin, which is selfishness. To see Christ as the true Son of God and the brother of all men, is to be sure that the soul is free, and that God is good, and that the end of life is noble service.

This is the message that I wanted to deliver in this book, as the true gospel for an age of doubt.

The title has been misunderstood by some of the critics who have read it, apparently without going any further into the book. They have

taken it as if it were an arraignment of the
present age for irreligion and infidelity. They
have resented it as if it were a confession of
the decline of Christianity. They have found
fault with the writer for a want of sympathy
with the intellectual perplexities of the men
and women of to-day, and a lack of insight into
their spiritual life and moral purposes.

It seems strange that any one should make
such a criticism. The answer to it may be
found in the first chapter, where I have tried
to draw the distinction between doubt and
infidelity. But in order that there may be no
room for mistake, I will say what I mean again,
and yet more clearly.

In calling the present "an age of doubt," I
do not mean that it is the only age in which
doubt has been prevalent, nor that doubt is the
only characteristic of the age. I mean simply
that it is one of those periods of human history
in which the sudden expansion of knowledge
and the breaking-up of ancient moulds of
thought have produced a profound and wide-
spread feeling of uncertainty in regard to the
subject of religion. The remarkable achievements of the critical method as applied to
philosophy, history, and literature, have led
men to ask whether it may not be applied in

the same way to theology, and to take it for
granted that the result must be destructive.
The difficulty of adjusting the new discoveries
of science to the established forms of theological doctrine, has produced in some reluctant
and irritable minds a disposition to resent all
scientific research, and to denounce it as atheistic. But in a far greater number of minds it
has begotten a misgiving, that if religion needs
to defend itself by denying facts it must stand
on a very insecure foundation. There is a
large class of people, thoughtful, earnest, sincere, who live under the shadow of this
misgiving. They want religion. They are
attracted by its spiritual ideals, by its moral
inspiration. But they hesitate to accept it,
at least in its Christian form, for fear that
it may not be reasonable. The questioning
temper holds possession of their minds. Their
attitude toward religious things is interroga-
tive. The secular spirit insensibly gains dominion over their thoughts and feelings.
They grow weary of asking questions which
seem to find no answer. The influence of the
great mass of popular literature in which
religion is practically ignored, tends to foster
the impression that it is a subject in regard to
which certainty is neither necessary nor attain-

able. The existence of God, the reality of
the soul, the prospect of immortality, — these
appear like insoluble problems to many of the
children of this age. They are troubled and
depressed and impoverished by the want of
faith, but they accept indecision as the only
rational attitude, and try to do the best that
they can without believing in

"The truths that never can be proved."

This is what I mean by an age of doubt.
Who that knows the young men and women of
to-day, can deny that multitudes of the very
best of them are feeling the influence of this
kind of doubt, and suffering under it? Who
can fail to see that in many ways this kind of
doubt is an evidence of spiritual sincerity, of
moral earnestness, of a desire to be true to the
truth at all costs? Who can forget that the
sadness, the despondency, the pessimism of
many of those who have surrendered faith at
the call of what they conceived to be an intellectual duty, is in itself a proof that religion is
necessary to complete human life and make the
world endurable?

This is a doubting age. But it is not therefore an age to be despised or despaired of. It
is a hopeful age, an earnest age, an age of gen-

erous feeling and noble action. What it needs is a clear answer to its doubt, and a powerful remedy for its sadness. This answer and this remedy are found in the person of Jesus Christ. His life is a fact which cannot be explained without God. His character is a standing proof of the reality of the spiritual world. A universe of matter and force could never have produced such a person. His teaching is a direct witness to things which are unseen and eternal. Those who will receive it shall find His words a fountain of living waters springing up within them unto everlasting life.

It is not to be supposed that any one can write or speak so as to make everybody perceive and accept this truth. All human preaching comes far short of the fulness of the gospel. Even while Christ was on earth there were many who doubted, and held fast to their doubts. But I am sure that the most helpful, the most convincing message for a doubtful age is that which centres in His person, and seeks to make Him evident as the final and immutable revelation of God.

That is what this book tries to do. It is in fact nothing more than an endeavour to prove these two things: Christ is a real person; Christ is God manifest in the flesh.

But it differs from other arguments for the Divinity of Christ in at least one point. It accepts without reserve or qualification the perfect humanity of Christ. The chapter in which this view of the person of Jesus is expressed has been criticised as dangerous. I cannot alter it, because it represents my most profound convictions. To me it seems not dangerous, but safe, — far more safe, indeed, than any other view, because it corresponds more closely with the facts. The life which Christ lived on earth was a veritable human life. The person who lived it was the Son of God. But in order to live that human life He had to become man, not in a dramatic sense, but actually and entirely. There were not two wills and two minds working within the person of Jesus. The mind that was in Christ was a single mind, and His will was the expression of an undivided personality. He was subject to ignorance, to limitation, to weakness, to temptation, even as we are. The only point of difference between Him and us is that we sin, but He sinned not. The Godhood that was in Him was such as manhood is capable of receiving. There is no evidence in His life or in His character of the omniscience and omnipresence and omnipotence that would have separated

Him from us. His existence among men was simply the human life of God.

It seems to me that this is the view of Christ which is given in the New Testament. I have tried to express it clearly, because it opens the way to the dissolving of many doubts, and makes His Divinity at once easier to be believed, in and more precious in its significance. And if it does this for one reader who has been troubled by unbelief in the Divinity of Christ, if it shows one seeker after God how to find Him in the man Christ Jesus, the chief purpose of the book will be accomplished.

The same considerations and desires have controlled my treatment of the doctrines of foreordination, sovereignty, and election. There has been no intention to enter into theological controversy. Indeed, if I had intended to do this, the report of the critics upon the result would fill me with curious confusion. For they seem to be unable to decide upon which side of the controversy the book is to be reckoned. One of them calls it "a violent and unfair attack upon Calvinism"; another says that "it presents the doctrines of the Westminster Confession so winningly that they are accepted almost before they are recognized."

The compliment and the reproach are alike undeserved. In point of fact I was not thinking at all of Calvinism or of the Westminster Confession, but only of the New Testament, and of how directly it meets the wants of our age with the liberating teachings of Christ. Nothing has been more effective in begetting and increasing doubts than the idea that Christian doctrine required us to believe that all events, good and evil, were foreordained by God, and that some men were eternally chosen to be saved, without regard to their faith or works, while all the rest were left to inevitable destruction. There is no trace of such an idea in the mind of Christ. On the contrary, He is the great liberator of men from the bondage of fatalism, and His invitation to all the weary and heavy-laden to come unto Him is a divine assurance that whosoever will may have everlasting life.

After years of doubt and inward conflict I have arrived at great peace and comfort in the unreserved acceptance of these teachings of Jesus. I do not believe that all things that happen are determined beforehand. The soul is free. The evil that men do is all their own; God has not foreordained it. His only predestination is to good, and if men will accept

their divine destiny, God will help them to fulfil
it.   Election is not the arbitrary choice of a
few to receive blessings from which the many
are excluded.   It is the selection of certain
races and men to receive great privileges to fit
them for the service of all mankind in the
divine kingdom.   This is my faith in regard to
these questions.   I have made no secret of it.
The recent agitation concerning ministerial
honour in creed subscription seemed to require
that it should be frankly confessed.   If such a
faith were inconsistent with any ecclesiastical
obligations, I should be prompt to renounce
them.   But it is evident that there is no incon-
sistency.   A man may hold this faith and
preach it, as a loyal Christian, in the fellowship of the Presbyterian Church.

It remains only to add a word of explanation
in regard to a criticism of this book which goes
deeper than any of those of which I have
spoken.   A writer, for whose opinion I have
great respect, has said that the volume does
not give due place and proportion to the truth
of the Atonement ; that it fails to set forth
Christ as "the Lamb of God which taketh
away the sin of the world."

If this were altogether true, I should be very

sorry. I certainly believe that Christ is the only Saviour of sinners; that He died to redeem men from the curse of sin, and that the attraction of His cross is most potent upon the human heart. I have tried to say this very distinctly in the second chapter and at the close of the fourth chapter.

But that the criticism is partly true I must admit. The Atonement does not appear in its due place and proportion in this book. It would not have been possible without prolonging the volume to a much greater length and turning aside from the purpose for which it was written. It was not intended to be a complete statement of Christian truth. It was meant only to present that aspect of the gospel which seemed to be especially adapted to the wants of an age of doubt. I was thinking of the men and women whose minds are confused and troubled by modern speculations, who are oppressed by the intellectual difficulties of belief, who feel the benumbing influence of the secular spirit, and who stand sadly in doubt in regard to the reality of the whole spiritual life. I wanted to say something to help them, something to make it easier for them to believe in Christ, and, through Christ, in God.

I know very well that it is not enough for

men to be delivered from doubt. They need also to be saved from sin. But before this can have any meaning to them they must begin to believe in a Divine Being and in their own spiritual relationship to Him. What does sin mean to a man who doubts whether there is a personal God, and thinks that his soul may be only a name for a certain secretion of the gray matter in his brain, and has no sure expectation of a life beyond death? What he needs first of all is a gospel which will bring him news of a real spiritual world, a gospel whose simplicity and directness and personal force will make the first adventure of faith possible. It was of such men as this that I was thinking, when this book was written.

I know very well that the book is incomplete. It touches only one aspect of the greatest of all subjects. It needs a sequel, to make it harmonize more fully with the truth as it is in Jesus, and to bring it into touch with another side of the need of humanity. Very soon, I hope to be permitted to follow this volume on "The Gospel for an Age of Doubt," with another, on "The Gospel for a World of Sin."

"Thule," York Harbour,
July 10th, 1898.

CONTENTS

1

AN AGE OF DOUBT

"Cleave ever to the sunnier side of doubt,
    And cling to Faith beyond the forms of Faith!
    She reels not in the storm of warring words,
    She brightens at the clash of 'Yes' and 'No,'
    She sees the Best that glimmers thro' the Worst,
    She feels the Sun is hid but for a night,
    She spies the summer thro' the winter bud,
    She tastes the fruit before the blossom falls,
    She hears the lark within the songless egg,
    She finds the fountain where they wail'd 'Mirage'!"
                    — TENNYSON, *The Ancient Sage.*

AN AGE OF DOUBT

THERE is one point in which all men resem- *The person-al equation of the age.* ble each other : it is that they are all different. But their differences are not fixed and immutable. They are variable and progressive. Types of character survive or perish, like the forms of animal life. Some predominate ; others are subordinated.

Thus it comes to pass that underneath all the diversities of individual life, we may discern, not with the clearness of a portrait, but with the vague outlines of a composite photograph, the features of a *Zeitgeist*, a spirit of the time. Generations differ almost as much as the men who compose them. There is a personal equation in every age.

To know this is a necessity for the preacher. Even as the physician must apprehend the idiosyncrasy of his patient, and the teacher must recognize the quality of his pupil, so must the preacher be in touch with his age.

In endeavouring to arrive at this knowledge, contact with the world is of the first consequence. For one who desires to make men and women what they ought to be, nothing can take the place of an acquaintance with men and women as they are. It seems to me that one of the best means of obtaining this acquaintance is through literature, — not that highly specialized and more or less technical variety of literature which is produced expressly for certain classes of readers, but literature in the broader sense, as it appeals to cultivated and intelligent people in general, including contemporary history and criticism, poetry and fiction, popular philosophy and diluted science. This kind of literature is the efflorescence of the Zeitgeist. It is at once a product, and a cause, of the temperament of the age. In it we see not only what certain men have written by way of comment on the movement of the times, but also what a great many men are reading while they move. It expresses, and it creates, a spirit, an attitude of mind. "I do not imagine," says a keen observer, "that I am announcing an altogether novel truth in affirming that literature is one of the elements of the ethical life, — the most important perhaps; for in the decline, more and more evident, of traditional and local influences, the book is taking its place as the great initiator." [1]

For this reason I believe that a course in modern novels and poetry might well be made a part of every scheme of preparation for the ministry. The preacher who does not know what his people are reading does not know his people. He will miss the significance of the current talk of society, and even of the daily comments of the newspapers, which are in fact only a cheap substitute for conversation, unless he has the key to it in the tone of popular literature. It is from this source that I have drawn many of the illustrations for this lecture. If they appear unfamiliar or out of place in a theological seminary, I can only say that they seem to me none the less, but perhaps the more, significant and valuable on that account. For I think that one of the causes by which, as John Foster wrote seventy years ago, "Evangelical Religion has been rendered unacceptable to persons of cultivated taste," [2] has been a certain ill-disguised contempt on the part of

The value of general reading.

[1] Paul Bourget, *Essais de Psychologie Contemporaine*, Paris, 1895.

[2] John Foster, *Essays*, " On the Aversion of Men of Taste to Evangelical Religion," p. 188.

persons of orthodox opinions for what they are pleased to call, "mere *belles-lettres*." And though I do not fancy that there is any sympathy with that frame of mind in this place, yet the occasion seems opportune for saying in a definite way that the preacher who wishes to speak to this age must read many books in order that he may be in a position to make the best use of what Sir Walter Scott called "the one Book." He must keep himself in touch with modern life by studying modern literature, which is one of its essential factors.

I

A doubting age.

As soon as we step out of the theological circle into the broad field of general reading we see that we are living in an age of doubt.

I do not mean to say that this is the only feature in the physiognomy of the age. It has many other aspects, from any one of which we might pick a name. From the material side, we might call it an age of progress; from the intellectual side, an age of science; from the medical side, an age of hysteria; from the political side, an age of democracy; from the commercial side, an age of advertisement; from the social side, an age of publicomania.

But looking at it from the spiritual side, which is the preacher's point of view, and considering that interior life to which every proclamation of a gospel must be addressed, beyond a doubt it stands confessed as a doubting age.

There is a profound and wide-spread unsettlement of soul in regard to fundamental truths of religion, and also in regard to the nature and existence of the so-called spiritual faculties by which alone these truths can be perceived. In its popular manifestations, this unsettlement takes the form of uncertainty rather than of denial, of unbelief rather than of disbelief, of general scepticism rather than of specific infidelity. The questioning spirit is abroad, moving on the face of the waters, seeking rest and finding none.

The questioning spirit.

It is not merely that particular doctrines, such as the inspiration of the Bible, or the future punishment of the wicked, are attacked and denied. The preacher who concentrates his attention at these points will fail to realize the gravity of the situation. It is not that a spirit of bitter and mocking atheism, such as Bishop Butler described at the close of the last century, has led people of discernment to set up religion "as a principal subject of

mirth and ridicule, as it were by way of reprisal for its having so long interrupted the
pleasures of the world."[1] The preacher who
takes that view of the case now will be at
least fifty years too late. He will fail to
understand the serious and pathetic temper of
the age.

Respectful unbelief.

The questioning spirit of to-day is severe
but not bitter, restless but not frivolous; it
takes itself very seriously and applies its methods of criticism, of analysis, of dissolution,
with a sad courtesy of demeanour, to the deepest and most vital truths of religion, the being
of God, the reality of the soul, the possibility
of a future life. Everywhere it comes and
everywhere it asks for a reason, in the shape
of a positive and scientific demonstration.
When one is given, it asks for another, and
when another is given, it asks for the reason
of the reason. The laws of evidence, the principles of judgment, the witness of history, the
testimony of consciousness, — all are called in
question. The answers which have been given
by religion to the most difficult and pressing
problems of man's inner life are declared to
be unsatisfactory and without foundation. The

[1] Joseph Butler, *The Analogy of Religion* (London, Bell
& Daldy, 1858). "Advertisement," p. xxiv.

question remains unsolved. Is it insoluble? The age stands in doubt. Its coat-of-arms is an interrogation point rampant, above three bishops dormant, and its motto is *Query?*

II

If we inquire the cause of this general scep- *Causes of scepticism.* ticism in regard to religion, the common answer from all sides would probably attribute it to the progress of science. I do not feel satisfied with this answer. At least I should wish to qualify it in such a way as to give it a very different meaning from that which is implied in the current phrase "the conflict between science and religion."

Science, in itself considered, the orderly and *Science not hostile to religion.* reasoned knowlêdge of the phenomenal universe of things and events, ought not to be, and has not been, hostile to religion, simply because it does not, and cannot, enter into the same sphere. The great advance which has been made in the observation and classification of sensible facts, and in the induction of so-called general laws under which those facts may be arranged for pur- poses of study, has not even touched the two questions upon the answer to which the reality and nature of religion depend : first, the possible existence of other facts which physical science cannot observe and classify; and second, the probable explanation of these facts. What has happened is just this. The field in which faith has to work has been altered, and it seems to me enormously broadened. But the work remains the same. The question is whether faith has enough vital energy to face and accomplish it. For example, the material out of which to construct an argument from the evidences of final cause in nature has been incalculably increased by the discoveries of the last fifty years in regard to natural selection and the origin of species. The observant wanderer in the field of nature to-day no longer stumbles upon Dr. Paley's old-fashioned, open-faced, turnip-shaped watch lying on the ground. He finds, instead, an intricate and self-adjusting chronometer, capable not only of marking time with accuracy, but also of evolving by its own operation another more perfect and delicate instrument, with qualities and powers which adapt themselves to their surroundings and so advance forever. The idea of final cause has not been touched. Only the region which it must illuminate has been vastly enlarged. It remains to be seen whether faith can supply the illuminating power. Already we have the

The task of faith not changed, but enlarged.

promise of an answer in many books, by masters of science and philosophy, who show that the theory of evolution demands for its completion the recognition of the spiritual nature of man and the belief in an intelligent and personal God.

The spread of scepticism is often attributed to the growth of our conception of the physical magnitude of the universe. The bewildering numbers and distances of the stars, the gigantic masses of matter in motion, and the tremendous sweep of the forces which drive our tiny earth along like a grain of dust in an orderly whirlwind, are supposed to have overwhelmed and stunned the power of spiritual belief in man. The account seems to me incorrect and unconvincing. I observe that precisely the same argument was used by Job and Isaiah and the Psalmists to lead to a conclusion of faith. The striking disproportion between the littleness of man and the greatness of the stars was to them a demonstration of the necessity of religion to solve the equation. They saw in the heavens the glory of God. And if man to-day knows vastly more of the heavens, does not that put him in position to receive a larger and loftier vision of the glory?

The expansion of knowledge.

We observe, moreover, that it is just in those departments of science where the knowledge of the magnitude and splendid order of the physical universe is most clear and exact, namely, in astronomy and mathematics, that we find the most illustrious men of science who have not been sceptics but sincere and steadfast believers in the Christian religion. Kepler and Newton were men of faith. The most brilliant galaxy of mathematicians ever assembled at one time and place was at the University of Cambridge in the latter half of this century. Of these " Sir W. Thomson, Sir George Stokes, Professors Tait, Adams, Clerk-Maxwell, and Cayley — not to mention a number of lesser lights, such as Routh, Todhunter, Ferrers, etc. — were all avowed Christians." [1] Surely it needs no further proof to show that the pursuit of pure science does not necessarily tend to scepticism.

The arrogance of science falsely so-called.

No, we must look more closely and distinguish more clearly in order to discover in the scientific activities of the age a cause of the prevailing doubt. And if we do this I think we shall find it in the fallacy of that kind of science which mistakes itself for omniscience.

[1] George John Romanes, M.A., LL.D., F.R.S., *Thoughts on Religion* (Chicago, 1895), p. 147.

" What we see is the pretence of certain sciences to represent in themselves all human knowledge. And as outside of knowledge there is no longer, in the eyes of science thus curtailed, any means for man to come in contact with the realities, we see the pretence advanced by some that all reality and all life should be reduced to that which they have verified. Outside of this there are only dreams and illusions. This is indeed too much. It is no longer science, but scientific absolutism."[1]

" The history of the natural sciences," said Du Bois-Reymond in 1877, " is the veritable history of mankind." " The world," says another, " is made of atoms and ether, and there is no room for ghosts." M. Berthelot in the preface to his *Origines de l'alchimie*, modestly claims that " the world to-day is without mysteries "; meaning thereby, I suppose, that there is nothing in existence, from the crystallization of a diamond to the character of a saint, which cannot be investigated and explained by means of a crucible, a blow-pipe, a microscope, and a few other tools.

This is simply begging the question of a spiritual world in the negative. It is an im-

An immense assumption.

[1] Charles Wagner, *Youth*, translated from the French by Ernest Redwood (New York, 1893), p. 28.

mense and stupefying assumption. It is a claim to solve the problems of the inner life by suppressing them. This claim is not in any sense necessary to the existence of science, nor to any degree supported by the work which it has actually accomplished. But it is made with a calm assurance which imposes powerfully upon the popular mind; and, being made in the name of science, it carries with it an appearance of authority borrowed from the great service which science has rendered to humanity by its discoveries in the sphere of the visible.

Results of this assumption.

The result of this *petitio principii* in the minds of those who accept it fully and carry it out to its logical conclusion, is a definite system of metaphysical negation which goes under the various names of Naturalism, Positivism, Empiricism, and Agnosticism. Its result in the minds of those who accept it partially and provisionally, but lack the ability or the inclination to formulate it, is the development of a sceptical temper. Its result in the minds of those who are unconsciously affected by it, through those profound instincts of sympathy and involuntary imitation which influence all men, is an attitude, — more or less sincere, more or less consistent and con-

tinuous, — an attitude of doubt. The spirit
of the age tacitly divides all the various
beliefs which are held among men into two
classes. Those which are supported by scientific proof must be accepted. Those which
are not thus supported either must be rejected, or may safely and properly be disregarded as matters of no consequence.

III

Now this general scepticism, in all its
shades and degrees, from the most clear, self-
conscious, and aggressive, to the most vague,
diffused, and deprecatory, is reflected in the
productions of current literature. Never was
literary art more perfect, more accomplished,
more versatile and successful than in the present age. Never have its laws been more widely
understood and its fascinations more potently
exercised. Never has it evoked more magical
and charming forms to float above an abyss
of disenchantment and nothingness.

*The mirror
of literature
and the
shadow of
doubt.*

In the lay sermons and essays of Huxley
and Tyndall and Frederic Harrison and W. K.
Clifford, scepticism appears militant and trench-
ant. These knights-errant of Doubting Castle
are brilliantly equipped as men of war; and

even when they fall foul of each other, as they often do, the ground of the conflict is an accusation of infidelity to the principles of unbelief, and its object is to drive the adversary back into a more complete and consistent negation.

Over the fragmentary but majestic life-philosophies of Carlyle and Emerson, lying in the disarray of stones hewn for a temple yet unbuilt, imaginative scepticism hangs like a cloud. Over Carlyle, it is the shadow of a noonday tempest, full of darkness and tumult and muttering thunder. Over Emerson, it floats like a cumulus of evening vapours, luminous and beautiful, alluringly transfigured

> "In the golden lightning
> Of the sunken sun." [1]

In the vivid and picturesque historical studies of Renan and Froude, scepticism is at once ironical and idealistic, destructive and dogmatic. In the penetrative and intelligent critiques of Scherer and Morley, it adheres with proud but illogical persistence to the ethical consequences of the faith with which logic has broken : like a son disinherited, but resolved to maintain the right of possession by the strong arm.

[1] Shelley, "Ode to a Skylark."

In the novels of unflinching and unblushing naturalism,—like those of Zola and Maupassant and the later works of Thomas Hardy, scepticism speaks with a harsh and menacing accent of the emptiness of all life and the futility of all endeavour. In the psychological romances of Flaubert and Bourget and Spielhagen, George Eliot and Mrs. Humphry Ward, it holds the mirror up to human nature to disclose a face darkened with inconsolable regret for lost dreams. Far apart as *Madame Bovary* and *Cosmopolis, Problematische Naturen* and *Middlemarch* and *Robert Elsmere* may be in many of their features, do they not wear the same expression, — the cureless melancholy of disillusion? *Fiction gloomy.*

Fiction in its more superficial form, dealing only with the manners and customs of the social drama, and relying for its interest mainly upon local colour and the charm of incident narrated with vivacity and grace, betrays its scepticism by a serene, unconscious disregard of the part which religion plays in real life. In how many of the lighter novels of the day do we find any recognition, even between the lines, of the influence which the idea of God or its absence, the practice of prayer or its neg-

c

lect, actually exercise upon the character and conduct of men? Take, for example, *Trilby*,[1] as the type of a clever book carelessly written for the thoughtless public of a passing moment. It is incredibly credulous in regard to the dramatic possibilities of hypnotism. It is pitifully inadequate in its conception of the actual potencies of religion ; and it uses Christianity chiefly as a subject for caricature in the style of the illustrated newspapers, which are called comic.

Poetry despondent.

Poetry has always been the most direct and intimate utterance of the human heart. And it is in poetry that we hear to-day the voice of scepticism most clearly, "making abundant music around an elementary nihilism, now stripped naked."[2] Listen to its sonorous chantings as they come from France in the verse of Leconte de Lisle, celebrating the sombre ritual of human automata before the altar of the unknown and almighty tyrant, who agitates them endlessly for his own amusement. Listen to its delicate and decadent lyrics, as Charles Baudelaire sings his defeat in life and his thirst for annihilation.

> "Morne esprit, autrefois amoureux de la lutte,
> L'Espoir dont l'éperon attisait ton ardeur

[1] George Du Maurier, *Trilby* (Harpers, 1895).
[2] Paul Desjardins, *Le Devoir Present* (Paris, 1892), p. 65.

Ne veut plus t'enfourcher. Couche toi sans pudeur,
Vieux cheval dont le pied à chaque obstacle butte.

Résigne-toi, mon cœur, dors ton sommeil de brute.

Et le Temps m'engloutit minute par minute
Comme la neige immense un corps pris de roideur :
Je contemple d'en haut le globe en sa rondeur
Et je n'y cherche plus l'abri d'une cahute !

Avalanche, veux tu m'emporter dans ta chute?" [1]

Turn to England and hear its musical confession in the cool, sad, melodious tones of
Matthew Arnold, no enemy of faith, but her
disenchanted lover.

> " Forgive me, masters of the mind,
>   At whose behest I long ago
>   So much unlearned, so much resigned —
> I come not here to be your foe;
> I seek these anchorites not in ruth,
> To curse and to deny your truth ;
>
> Not as their friend, or child, I speak
> But as on some far northern strand,
> Thinking of his own gods, a Greek,
> In pity and mournful awe might stand
> Before a fallen Runic stone, —
> For both were faiths, and both are gone." [2]

There is a poem by Tennyson (who never
broke with faith, though he felt the strain of

[1] Charles Baudelaire, *Fleurs du Mal* (Paris, 1888), p. 205.
" Le goût du Néant."
[2] Matthew Arnold, *Poems* (New York, Macmillan, 1878),
p. 337. " Stanzas from the Grande Chartreuse."

doubt), in which he describes with intense dramatic sympathy the finality of scepticism in the human soul. It is called "Despair." There is another poem, called "Sea Dreams," in which he gives a vision of the rising tide of doubt as it threatens to undermine and overwhelm the beliefs of the past. The woman is telling her husband the dream which came to her in the night as she watched by their sick child.

A picture of the sea of doubt.

> "But round the North, a light,
> A belt, it seem'd, of luminous vapour, lay,
> And ever in it a low musical note
> Swell'd up and died; and, as it swell'd, a ridge
> Of breaker issued from the belt, and still
> Grew with the growing note, and when the note
> Had reach'd a thunderous fulness, on those cliffs
> Broke, mixt with awful light (the same as that
> Living within the belt) whereby she saw
> That all those lines of cliffs were cliffs no more,
> But huge cathedral fronts of every age,
> Grave, florid, stern, as far as eye could see,
> One after one: and then the great ridge drew,
> Lessening to the lessening music, back,
> And passed into the belt and swell'd again
> Slowly to music: ever when it broke
> The statues, king, or saint, or founder, fell;
> Then from the gaps and chasms of ruin left
> Came men and women in dark clusters round,
> Some crying, 'Set them up! they shall not fall!'
> And others, 'Let them lie, for they have fall'n.'
> And still they strove and wrangled: . . .
>   . . . and ever as their shrieks

Ran highest up the gamut, that great wave
Returning, while none mark'd it, on the crowd
Broke, mixt with awful light, and show'd their eyes
Glaring, and passionate looks, and swept away
The men of flesh and blood, and men of stone,
To the waste deeps together." [1]

It was but a dream, dispelled from the mind *The pity of it.*
of her to whom it came in the night-watches
by the crying of her little child, and soon forgotten in the sweet reality of human love.
Only a dream, but how many souls have felt
the vague sadness, the haunting, helpless pity
and fear of a like vision, looking out upon the
landscape of man's inner life, and seeing the
ancient landmarks slowly melted or swiftly
swept away, the shrines of memory shaken
and removed, the fair images of immortal desire and aspiration dissolving and disappearing
in the onward waves, silently creeping, or surg-
ing with mysterious and inarticulate music out
of the waste deep of doubt, —

"The unplumbed, salt, estranging sea." [2]

Who can think of the sharp anguish and dull
grief that have fallen upon innumerable hearts
through the loss of their most precious faiths ;

[1] Tennyson's *Poetical Works* (Macmillan, 1890), p. 138.
[2] Matthew Arnold, "To Marguerite." *Poems* (Macmillan, 1878), p. 184.

who can think of the gray, formless, ever-moving, yet immovable flood of mordant gloom that has covered so many once bright and fertile fields of human hope and endeavour, so many once secure and peaceful homes of human trust and confidence, — who can think of these things, even though his own standpoint be still untouched, his own faith-dwelling founded upon an untrembling rock far above the tide, without a sorrowful perturbation of spirit and a deep, inward sense of compassionate distress and dread ?   We stand upon the shore, but we stand beside the sea.   And we look out upon it, as Émile Littré sadly wrote,[1] like the women of Troy, whom the Roman poet pictured gazing at its mighty currents and engulfing waves:

"Pontum adspectabant flentes."

IV

Sympathy with doubt.   It is with no careless and exaggerating hand, it is in no unsympathetic and condemning spirit, that I have tried to draw this picture of the sceptical age in which we live.   Its faults, its perils, are mine and yours.   The preacher who assumes a supercilious and damnatory attitude

[1] Émile Littré, *Conservation, Révolution, Positivisme, Remarques,* p. 430.

towards the doubts of the present time can do little to relieve, and may do much to increase them. If we desire to be true ministers to a doubting age, we must put ourselves in the position of Maurice, who said, "I wish to confess the sins of the time as my own."[1] So far as current scepticism has its source in evil, it flows from faults of which we all partake, — the pride of intellect, the haste of judgment, the preference of the seen to the unseen, the impatience of ignorance, the vain demand of perfection in the finite comprehension of the infinite, and the disloyalty of reason to conscience.

But indeed this is not the point of view from which we speak. This lecture is not an indictment. It is a diagnosis. Doubt, as we are thinking of it, is not a crime, but a malady. And if we are to have any hope or power of staying its progress and healing its ravages, we must not only be sympathetic in our understanding of it, but we must also look through it, earnestly and patiently, to see whether there are not some favourable symptoms, some signs of enduring vitality, some promises of returning health and strength in the spirit of the age.

Lessons of encouragement.

Of these it seems to me that there are three,

[1] *The Life of Frederick Denison Maurice* (New York, Scribners, 1884), vol. ii., p. 235.

so evident and so important, that we ought not to overlook them. First, the acknowledged discontent and pain of unbelief; second, the practical recoil of some of the finest minds from the void of absolute scepticism; third, the persistent desire of many doubting spirits to serve mankind by love, self-sacrifice, and ethical endeavour. In other words, I would read the lesson of encouragement in the sufferings of doubt, in the doubts of doubt, and in the splendid moral inconsistencies of doubt.

Pessimism. Begin, then, with pain, which is not only a warning of disease, but also a sign of life. The pessimism which goes hand in hand with scepticism in this nineteenth century is a cry of suffering. The closely reasoned philosophies of Schopenhauer and Hartmann, with their premisses of misery and conclusions of despair, are only the scientific statement of a widely diffused sentiment of dissatisfaction and despondency in regard to life.[1] Their spread, like that of some apparently new disease, is due to the fact that they give a name to something from which men have long suffered.

Cheerful scepticism almost-extinct. It seemed at one time as if the course of modern scepticism was to be free from sadness, a painless malady. At the beginning of the

[1] James Sully, *Pessimism*, pp. 2, 3.

century the tone of infidelity was jubilant and triumphant. Percy Bysshe Shelley walked into the inn at Montanvert and wrote his name in the visitors' book, adding "democrat, philanthropist, atheist,"—as if it were a record of victory and a title of glory. This cheerful type of scepticism still survives, here and there, in a few men who insist that the process of disenchantment is pleasant and joyous, and that the optimism which belonged to faith may remain while the faith itself disappears. It is like the smile of the famous cat, in the child's story-book, which broadened and brightened while the cat faded, until finally the animal was gone and nothing but the grin was left.

But for the most part modern doubt shows a sad and pain-drawn face, heavy with grief and dark with apprehension. There is an illustration of this change in the life of George Eliot. In her girlhood she passed suddenly, by an unconditional surrender, out of a warm faith in Evangelical Christianity into the coldest kind of rational scepticism. She writes of the dull, and now forgotten, book which wrought this change, Charles Hennell's *Inquiry concerning the Origin of Christianity*, with strange and almost fantastic merriment: "Mr. Hennell ought to be one of the happiest of men that he has

The sorrow of losing faith.

done such a life's work. I am sure if I had written such a book I should be invulnerable to all the arrows of all the gods and goddesses. The book is full of wit to me. It gives me that exquisite kind of laughter which comes from the gratification of the reasoning faculties."[1] But the arrows which she despised struck home, ere life was ended, to her own heart.

"I remember," writes Mr. F. W. H. Myers, "how at Cambridge I walked with her once in the Fellows' Garden of Trinity, on an evening of rainy May, and she, stirred somewhat beyond her wont, and taking as her text the three words which have been used so often as the inspiring trumpet-calls of men, — the words God, Immortality, Duty, — pronounced, with terrible earnestness, how inconceivable was the first, how unbelievable was the second, and how peremptory and absolute the third. Never, perhaps, had sterner accents affirmed the sovereignty of impersonal and unrecompensing law. I listened and night fell; her grave, majestic countenance turned towards me like a Sibyl's in the gloom; it was as though she withdrew from my grasp, one by one, the two scrolls of promise, and

[1] *George Eliot's Life, as related in her Letters* (New York, Harpers), vol. i., p. 119.

left me the third scroll only, awful with inevitable fate." [1]

An inevitable fate, seen through the gloom
of falling night, — that indeed is the aspect of
life which the literature of doubt displays to
us. A gray shadow of melancholy spreads
over the questioning, uncertain, disillusioned
age ; languid sighs of weariness breathe from
its salons and palaces. Bitter discontent mut-
ters in its workshops and tenements. "Never,
I believe," says Paul Desjardins, "have men
been more universally sad than in the present
time." And then he adds, with keen insight,
"Our misery lies in feeling that we are less
men than we were sixty years ago." [2] Human
life has been unspeakably impoverished and
narrowed by the loss of faith. Comedy has
become tragic, and tragedy has grown mean
and sordid. [3] Men have lost the sound of a
Divine voice in the story of their existence
and learned to listen to it as

The sad as-
pect of life.

> "a tale
> Told by an idiot, full of sound and fury
> Signifying nothing."

---

[1] R. H. Hutton, *Modern Guides of English Thought*
(London, Macmillan, 1887), p. 262.

[2] *Le Devoir Present*, pp. 17, 19.

[3] See the plays of Ibsen: *Ghosts, A Doll's House, The
Wild Duck,* etc.

Love itself, the great purifier and ennobler, has
been transformed in the subtle analysis of sex-
ual passion, from the sea-born Venus, pure and
radiant with immortal youth, to a dirt-engen-
dered goddess, concealing her secret ugliness
with illusory and artificial charms, and presiding with malignant power over the lower currents of man's being, — a veritable Cloacina of
human life.[1]

*The mean-
ness of man.*   The thought of "the grandeur and misery
of man," as Pascal conceived it, was painful
but elevating. The conception of the insig-
nificance and misery of man as scepticism presents it, is painful and dispiriting. Born of
blind force and unconscious matter, quickened
by some mysterious cruelty to a consciousness
of his own origin and a foreboding of his inexplicable and fruitless destiny, he "drees his
weird," between two fathomless abysses of
gloom, as one who is indeed weary and heavy-
laden. The music with which he accompanies
his march towards the blank and dismal bourn,
rolls and clashes through the literature of every
land with deep and mournful discords, as if
man had at last invented that strange organ of

[1] Bourget, *Psychologie Contemporaine*, pp, 5, 8.

expression which a satirist has called "the *Mis-érophon*." [1]

"This philosophy," says Stendhal, comment- *The nausea* ing upon the last reflections of his hero in *Rouge et Noir*, "was perhaps true, but it was of such a nature as to make one long for death." And then the critic from whom I have quoted these words, adds his own commentary. "Do you perceive, at the close of this work, the most complete which the author has left, the break- ing of the tragic dawn of pessimism? It rises, this dawn of blood and tears, and, like the clear- ness of a new-born day, it overspreads with crimson hues the loftiest spirits of our age, those whose thoughts are at the summit, those to whom the eyes of the men of to-morrow lift themselves, — religiously. I am come in this series of psychological studies to the fifth and last of the personages whom I propose to ana- lyze. I have examined a poet, Baudelaire; a historian, Renan; a romancer, Flaubert; a philosopher, Taine; I have just examined one of these composite artists in whom the critic and the imaginative writer are closely united; and I have found in these five Frenchmen of

[1] Anton Bettelheim, article in *Cosmopolis*, January, 1896.

such importance, the same philosophy of disgust with the universal nothingness."[1]

Melancholia. If we turn to Russia, which has given us some of the most brilliant and influential, though undisciplined, writers of modern fiction, do we not hear, in an accent harsher and more formidable, the same conclusions, the same cries of nausea over the inextricable confusion and vain efforts of human life? If we turn to England, do we not see the same cloud of melancholy, less threatening, less angry, but no less dark, rising from the chasm which doubt has made between man's inner life and the world as scientific positivism pictures it? How mournful is the voice in which W. K. Clifford proclaims, " The Great Companion is dead!" How dark with silent, passionate grief is that lonely wood in which " Robert Elsmere " feels himself going blind to the dearest visions of his former faith.[2] How black the air in which " Jude the Obscure " breathes out the last throbbings of his insurgent heart in curses upon his sordid and desperate fate![3] Let a

[1] Paul Bourget, *Psychologie Contemporaine*, p. 321.

[2] Mrs. Humphry Ward, *Robert Elsmere* (Macmillan, 1888), vol. ii., chap. xxvi.

[3] Thomas Hardy, *Jude the Obscure* (Harpers, 1896).

poet, with that sublime insight of genius
which endures even amid the ruins created
by its own destructive passion, speak the
last word of doubt, — the epitaph of *The
City of Dreadful Night*. The portentous figure of "Melancholia" sits enthroned above her
vast metropolis.

> " The moving Moon and stars from east to west
>   Circle before her in the sea of air;
>   Shadows and gleams glide round her solemn rest.
>   Her subjects often gaze up to her there:
>   The strong to drink new strength of iron endurance,
>   The weak, new terrors; all, renewed assurance
>   And confirmation of the old despair." [1]

But why despair, unless indeed because
man, in his very nature and inmost essence,
is framed for an immortal hope? No other
creature is filled with disgust and anger by
the mere recognition of its own environment
and the realization of its own destiny. This
strange issue of a purely physical evolution
in a profound revolt against itself is incredibly miraculous. Can a vast universe of atoms
and ether, unfolding out of darkness into darkness, produce at some point in its progress,
and that point apparently the highest, a feeling of profound disappointment with its par-

*Pain gives
an argu-
ment of
hope.*

[1] James Thomson, *The City of Dreadful Night*, xxi. 12.

tially discovered processes and resentful grief
at its dimly foreseen end? To believe this
would require a monstrous credulity! Atheism does not touch this difficulty. Agnosticism evades it. There are but two solutions
which really face the facts. One is the black,
unspeakable creed that the source of all things
is an unknown, mocking, malignant Power,
whose last and most cruel jest is the misery
of disenchanted man.[1] The other is the hopeful creed that the very pain which man suffers
when his spiritual nature is denied, is proof
that it exists, and part of the discipline by
which a truthful, loving God would lead man
to Himself. Let the world judge which is
the more reasonable faith. But for our part,
while we cling to the creed of hope, let us
not fail to "cleave ever to the sunnier side
of doubt," and see in the very shadow that
it casts the evidence of a light behind and
above it. Let us learn the meaning of that
noble word of St. Augustine : *Thou hast made
us for Thyself, and unquiet is our heart until it
rests in Thee.*

---

[1] "It must have been an ill-advised God, who could fall
upon no better amusement than the transforming of Himself
into such a hungry world as this, which is utterly miserable and
worse than none at all." — David Friedrich Strauss, quoted
in *The British Quarterly Review*, January, 1877, p. 146.

Yes, the inquietude of the heart which doubt has robbed of its faith in God, is an evidence that scepticism is a malady, not a normal state. The sadness of our times under the pressure of positive disbelief and negative uncertainty has in it the promise and potency of a return to health and happiness. Already we can see, if we look with clear eyes, the signs of what I have dared to call "the reaction out of the heart of a doubting age towards the Christianity of Christ and the faith in Immortal Love." [1]

Pagan poets, full of melancholy beauty and vague regret for lost ideals, poets of decadence and despondence, the age has born, to sing its grief and gloom. But its two great singers, Tennyson and Browning, strike a clearer note of returning faith and hope. "They resume the quest, and do not pause until they find Him whom they seek." [2] Pessimists like Hartmann work back unconsciously, from the vague remoteness of pantheism, far in the direction, at least, of a theistic view of the universe. His later books — *Religionsphilosophie* and

The renaissance of faith.

---

[1] *The Poetry of Tennyson* (New York, Scribners, 1889), p. xiii.

[2] Vida D. Scudder, *The Life of the Spirit in the Modern English Poets* (Houghton, Mifflin, & Co., 1895), p. 333.

D

Selbstersetzung des Christenthums — breathe a different spirit from his *Philosophie des Un-bewussten*.[1] One of the most cautious of our younger students of philosophy has noted with care, in a recent article, the indications that "the era of doubt is drawing to a close."[2] A statesman, like Signor Crispi, does not hesitate to cut loose from his former atheistic connections and declare that "the belief in God is the fundamental basis of the healthy life of the people, while atheism puts in it the germ of an irreparable decay." The French critic, M. Edouard Rod, declares that "only religion can regulate at the same time human thought and human action."[3] Mr. Benjamin Kidd, from the side of English sociology, assures us that "since man became a social creature, the development of his intellectual character has become subordinate to the development of his religious character," and concludes that religion affords the only permanent sanction for progress.[4] A famous biologist, Romanes,

[1] James Orr, *The Christian View of God and the World* (New York, Randolph, 1893), pp. 456, 457.

[2] *The Methodist Review*, January, 1896. "The Return to Faith," by Prof. A. C. Armstrong, Jr.

[3] Edouard Rod, *Les Idées Morales du Temps Present* (Paris, 1894), p. 304.

[4] Benjamin Kidd, *Social Evolution* (London, 1894), p. 245.

who once professed the most absolute rejection of revealed, and the most unqualified scepticism of natural, religion, thinks his way soberly back from the painful void to a position where he confesses that "it is reasonable to be a Christian believer," and dies in the full communion of the church of Jesus.[1]

All along the line, we see men who once thought it necessary or desirable to abandon forever the soul's abode of faith in the unseen, returning by many and devious ways from the far country of doubt, driven by homesickness and hunger to seek some path which shall at least bring them in sight of a Father's house.

And meanwhile we hear the conscience, the ethical instinct of mankind, asserting itself with splendid courage and patience, even in those who have as yet found no sure ground for it to stand upon. There is a sublime contradiction between the positivist's view of man as "the hero of a lamentable drama played in an obscure corner of the universe, in virtue of blind laws, before an indifferent nature, and with annihilation for its denouement,"[2] and the doctrine that it is his supreme duty to sacrifice himself for the good of humanity. Yet many

The indomitable conscience.

---

[1] *Thoughts on Religion*, p. 196.
[2] Madame L. Ackermann, *Ma Vie* (Paris, 1885), p. xviii.

of the sceptical thinkers of the age do not stumble at the contradiction. They hold fast to love and justice and moral enthusiasm even though they suspect that they themselves are the products of a nature which is blind and dumb and heartless and stupid. Never have the obligations of self-restraint, and helpfulness, and equity, and universal brotherhood been preached more fervently than by some of the English agnostics.

The new crusade in France.

In France a new crusade has risen; a crusade which seeks to gather into its hosts men of all creeds and men of none, and which proclaims as its object the recovery of the sacred places of man's spiritual life, the holy land in which virtue shines forever by its own light, and the higher impulses of our nature are inspired, invincible, and immortal. On its banner M. Paul Desjardins writes the word of Tolstoi, "*Il faut avoir une âme;* it is necessary to have a soul," and declares that the crusaders will follow it wherever it leads them. "For my part," he cries, "I shall not blush certainly to acknowledge as sole master the Christ preached by the doctors. I shall not recoil if my premisses force me to believe, at last, as Pascal believed." [1]

[1] *Le Devoir Present*, 45.

In our own land such a crusade does not yet appear to be necessary. The disintegration of faith under the secret processes of general scepticism has not yet gone far enough to make the peril of religion evident, or to cause a new marshalling of hosts to recover and defend the forsaken shrines of man's spiritual life. When the process which is now subtly working in so many departments of our literature has gone farther, it may be needful to call for such a crusade. If so, I believe it will come. I believe that the leaders of thought, the artists, the poets of the future, when they stand face to face with the manifest results of negation and disillusion, which really destroy the very sphere in which alone art and poetry can live, will rise to meet the peril, and proclaim anew with one voice the watchword, " It is necessary to have a soul! And though a man gain the whole world, if his soul is lost, it shall profit him nothing." But meanwhile, before the following of the errors of France in literature and art has led us to that point of spiritual impoverishment where we must imitate the organized and avowed effort to recover that which has been lost, we see a new crusade of another kind: a powerful movement of moral enthusiasm, of self-sacrifice, of altruism, even among

The new crusade in America.

those who profess to be out of sympathy with Christianity, which is a sign of promise, because it reveals a force that cries out for faith, and for Christian faith, to guide and direct it.

The cry for a gospel of leadership.

Never was there a time when the fine aspirations of the young manhood and young womanhood of our country needed a more inspiring and direct Christian leadership. The indications of this need lie open to our sight on every side. Here is a company of refined and educated people going down to make a college settlement among the poor and ignorant, to help them and lift them up. They declare that it is not a religious movement, that there is to be no preaching connected with it, that the only faith which it is to embody is faith in humanity. They choose a leader who has only that faith. But they find, under his guidance, that the movement will not move, that the work cannot be done, that it faints and fails because it lacks the spring of moral inspiration which can come only from a divine and spiritual faith. And they are forced to seek a new leader who, although he is not a preacher, yet carries within his heart that power of religious conviction, that force of devotion to the will of God, that faith in the living and supreme Christ, which is in fact the centre of Christianity. All around the circle of human doubt and despair, where men and women are going out to enlighten and uplift and comfort and strengthen their fellow-men under the perplexities and burdens of life, we hear the cry for a gospel which shall be divine, and therefore sovereign and unquestionable and sure and victorious. All through the noblest aspirations and efforts and hopes of our age of doubt, we feel the longing, and we hear the demand, for a new inspiration of Christian faith.

These are the signs of the times. Surely we must take note of them, surely we must labour and pray to understand their true significance, if we are to say anything to our fellow-men which shall be worth our saying and their hearing.

The signs of the times.

Renan made a strange remark not long before his death: "I fear that the work of the Twentieth Century will consist in taking out of the waste-basket a multitude of excellent ideas which the Nineteenth Century has heedlessly thrown into it." The sceptic's fear is the believer's hope. Once more the fields are white unto the harvest. The time is ripe; ripe in the sorrow of scepticism, ripe in the return of aspiration, ripe in the enthusiasm of humanity, for a renaissance of the spiritual life.

Already the horizon brightens with the tokens of this renaissance. There is a new interest in religion as the most living of all topics. There is a new sense of its vital meaning for the whole life of man. There is a new determination to apply it all around the circle of human responsibilities and test its value everywhere. There is a new cry for a Christ who shall fulfil the hopes of all the ages. There is a new love waiting for Him, a new devotion ready to follow His call. Doubt, in its nobler aspect, — honest, unwilling, morally earnest doubt, — has been a John the Baptist to prepare the way for His coming. The men of to-day are saying, as certain Greeks said to apostles of old, "Sirs, we would see Jesus." The disciple who can lead the questioning spirits to Him, is the man who has the Gospel for an Age of Doubt.

II

THE GOSPEL OF A PERSON

Subtlest thought shall fail and learning falter,
   Churches change, forms perish, systems go,
But our human needs, they will not alter,
   Christ no after age shall e'er outgrow.

Yea, Amen! O changeless One, Thou only,
   Art life's guide and spiritual goal,
Thou the Light across the dark vale lonely, —
   Thou the eternal haven of the soul.

                  — JOHN CAMPBELL SHAIRP.

II

THE GOSPEL OF A PERSON

THE prevalence and the quality of modern doubt, with its discontent and sadness, its self-misgivings and reactions, its moral inconsistencies and fine enthusiasms, bring the preacher who is alive and in earnest, face to face with the most important question of his life. What can I do, what ought I to do, as a preacher, to meet the strange, urgent, complicated needs of such a time as this?

How shall we serve the present age?

First of all, as a man, — and every preacher ought to be a man, though not every man is bound to be a preacher — as a man, it is necessary to lead a clean, upright, steadfast, useful life, purged from all insincerity, and lifted above all selfishness, and especially above that form of religious selfishness which is the besetting peril of those who feel themselves rich in faith in the midst of a generation that has been made poor by unbelief. Never has there been a time when character and conduct counted for

more than they do to-day. A life on a high
level, yet full of helpful, healing sympathy
for all life on its lowest levels, is the first debt
which we owe to our fellow-men in this age.

But beyond this, is there not something personal and specific which the conditions of the
present demand from us, as men who have not
only the common duty of living, but also the
peculiar vocation of speaking directly and constantly to the inner life of our brothers? We
want some distinct and definite message, which
is to be clearly formed in our thought and feeling and utterance, as the central, guiding, domi-
nating force in all our efforts to realize the fine
aspiration of the old hymn:

> " To serve the present age,
>   My calling to fulfil, —
> Oh, may it all my powers engage
>   To do my Master's will ! "

*Proposed
remedies
insufficient.*

Now the moment we look at the problem in
this light, we see that there are various lines
of activity open to us, and along all of these
lines men are making promises and prophecies
of usefulness and success. The cures which
are suggested for the malady of the age are
many and diverse. Of some of them we need
speak only in passing, to recognize that for
us, at least, they are unsuitable.

Herr Max Nordau, for example, in his curious and chaotic book, *Degeneration*, diagnoses the sickness of modern times as the result, not of a loss of faith, but of a fatal increase of nervous irritability produced by the strain of an intricate civilization. He declares that the malady must run its course, but that in time it will be healed by the restorative force of "*misoneism*, that instinctive, invincible aversion to progress and its difficulties that Lombroso has studied so much and to which he has given this name." [1]

The name is certainly not a pretty one, nor do I think that, after the first feeling of pleasure in learning to pronounce a newly imported word has passed, the contemplation of its meaning will afford us any profound sense of satisfaction or hope. The picture of mankind as a magnified Jemmy Button, returning from his temporary residence in England to his native *Terra del Fuego*, and flinging away his gloves and patent-leather shoes, to relapse into a peaceful and contented barbarism, is not inspiring. Who is there that would care to devote his life to the hastening of such a result? Who but the veriest quack, himself affected by the hysteria of the age, would think of curing

[1] Max Nordau, *Degeneration* (New York, 1895), p. 542.

the convulsions of St. Vitus' dance in an over-strained humanity by throwing the patient into the stupor of typhoid fever?

Psychical research.

Another and very different method of dealing with the malady of the times is suggested by those who believe that Science itself, in the immense future advance which is predicted for it, will supply the antidote for the scepticism which has accompanied its previous course. New discoveries will be made which will support the proposition: *Il faut avoir une âme.* New arguments will be constructed which will give us a scientific demonstration of the unseen universe and the future life. It is in this spirit that Mr. F. W. H. Myers calls attention to the phenomena of mesmerism and hypnotism and telepathy, and suggests that the need of the age is a more cordial and general interest in the investigations of the Society of Psychical Research.[1] I do not think, for one, that these investigations are to be slighted or despised. They may be of great value. But it is difficult to believe that this is the source to which the preacher is to look either for his inspiration or his message. For, in the first place, it is highly improbable that science is about to make any such aston-

[1] *Science and A Future Life* (Macmillan, 1893), pp. 34, 44.

ishing advance, either in methods or results, as some men anticipate. The best authorities admit this, and warn us that there are " limitations in the nature of the universe which must circumscribe the achievements of speculative research." [1] Mr. Myers himself makes the same admission, and says that so far as our discoveries are confined to the physical side of things, there is no ground whatever for sanguine hope. Moreover, in the second place, whatever work may be done in this direction must be accomplished, not by preachers, but by scientists. The average preacher has no particular vocation, and no adequate qualification, for the task. Neither by temperament nor by training is he fitted to judge of these matters. Now and then you will find a rare exception ; but as a rule nothing could be of less value than the scientific sermons of preachers who have only a bowing acquaintance with science. If the cure of modern scepticism is to be accomplished by the further progress of physical investigation, at least we must confess that this enterprise is not for us.

But there are two other ways of dealing with current doubt which demand closer attention. One of them is the philosophic

[1] C. H. Pearson, *National Life and Character* (Macmillan, 1893), p. 291.

method of a *reductio ad absurdum*. **The logic**
of rationalism is applied to its own premisses
in order to show that they are unfounded and
unverifiable. The result of this attack, as it
has been made with a relentless and masterly
hand by Mr. Arthur James Balfour in his
Defence of Philosophic Doubt, is to exhibit the
startling fact that "the universe as represented to us by science is wholly unimaginable,
and that our conception of it is what in Theology would be termed purely anthropomor-
phic."[1] The evidence for the existence of a
world composed of atoms and ether is no
more conclusive, the account which science
gives of their nature and qualities is no more
coherent, than the evidence and account which
faith gives of a world created by a personal
God and inhabited by immortal souls. Pure
agnosticism is thus forced into the service of
Christianity and used to destroy all *a priori*
objections to it. Giant Doubt is brought low
by turning his own weapons against himself,
even as Benaiah, the son of Jehoiada, slew the
Egyptian "with his own spear."[2]

The value of this service of philosophy is

---

[1] *A Defence of Philosophic Doubt* (Macmillan, 1879),
pp. 284, 285, 287–289.

[2] 1 Chron. xi. 23.

considerable. The Christian preacher ought
not to be ignorant of its actual results, for
they are such as to encourage him in preserving his independence against the tyrannous
claims of positivism ; nor unfamiliar with its
methods, for they are fitted to train and discipline his mind by hard exercise and exact work.
But it must be remembered that only a mighty
man of valour, one who, like Benaiah, ranks
above the host, and above the thirty captains of
the host, can hope to play a leading part in this
enterprise of " carrying the war into Africa."
It must be remembered also that the reduction
of scientific naturalism to an absurdity falls far
short of the establishment of religious faith as
a verity. Grateful for all that philosophy can
do, and is doing, to clear the way, the preacher
must have a principle, an impulse, a line of
action which will carry him beyond the negative result of making unbelief doubtful, to the
positive result of making belief credible.

At this point our attention is called to another way of dealing with current scepticism,
— the dogmatic method, which relies for the
defence of faith upon the construction of a
complete and consistent system of doctrine in
regard to God and man, the present world and
the future life. Faith, in other words, is to

*Theological
fortification.*

E

be established by fortification, surrounded and entrenched with banquette and parapet, scarp and ditch and counterscarp of iron-worded proof, defended on every side by solid syllogisms, and impregnable against all assaults of unbelief. It is foolish not to recognize the great work which has been done along this line by wise and strong men in the past. Those who affect to despise it and make light of it, are simply ignorant of some of the loftiest achievements of the human intellect. The works of Augustine and Anselm and Thomas Aquinas, of John Calvin and Richard Hooker and John Owen, of Ralph Cudworth and William Chillingworth, of Richard Baxter and Samuel Clarke and Joseph Butler, of Jonathan Edwards and Charles Hodge and W. G. T. Shedd, are massive works. They impose a sense of wonder upon every thoughtful observer.

Changed conditions. But concerning the attempt to conquer modern doubt by a system of dogmatic theology, certain things must be remembered. The conditions of warfare change from age to age. The vast fortresses of solid stone whose possession was once regarded as the security of nations, are not ranked so high as they were a hundred years ago. The earthwork, the rifled cannon, the iron-clad ship, the torpedo, have wrought great changes. Deductive logic is just as strong as it ever was, but somehow or other men are not as much impressed by it. Induction is the method of to-day: and that is a subtle, evasive, mobile method. It cannot be shut in by a ring of fortresses. Already the dogmatic systems in which the inductive method is ignored or subordinated (whether made long ago, or constructed yesterday on ancient models) are out of date. They are good for the men who are within them, but on the outside world they have no more effect than Windsor Castle would have in prctecting England from a foreign invasion.

We feel sure that theology, in time, must and will vindicate its claim to be considered as an essential factor in the intellectual life of man, by adapting itself to the changed conditions, and producing even mightier works by the new methods than those which it produced by the old. Already we see the promise of a renaissance of dogmatics in such books as Mulford's *The Republic of God*, Harris' *The Self-Revelation of God*, Orr's *The Christian View of God and the World*, and Fairbairn's *The Place of Christ in Modern Theology*. But we must remember that even those who anticipate and

The future of theology

Great things demanded of the new theologian. predict this reconstruction of the old truth on the new lines most enthusiastically, recognize that it must be a long and difficult task, and that the man who is to be a master-builder must have a magnificent equipment. How exhilarating at the first sight, but at the second sight how overwhelming and discouraging, are the demands of the age upon him who would fain be an epoch-making theologian, as they are stated, for example, in Mr. Balfour's *Foundations of Belief*, or in Dr. George A. Gordon's inspiring book *The Christ of To-day*. Truly it appears that such a man must realize the supposition of St. Paul: he must speak with the tongues of men and of angels, and have the gift of prophecy, and understand all mysteries and all knowledge. Who is sufficient for these things? It will take a long time for the best of us to learn all this. Perhaps the most of us may never go so far. Meantime, whether we are labouring towards that goal, or despairing of it, we need something divinely simple and divinely true that we can preach at once, directly, joyfully, fervently to the heart of the age.

A view of the world, a *Welt-anschauung*, is desirable, perhaps in the long run necessary, for the mind of man; but there is another thing which is more desirable and of prior necessity, and that is a standpoint of practical conviction from which to obtain such a view. It may be but a foothold, only a single point of contact, but we must have it, and it must be solid as a fact. A complete and consistent theology is a consummation most devoutly to be wished for; but before it can come there must be something else, — a living, active power of faith in the soul. This power, as we believe, already exists in every human being. But there is only one thing that can awaken it and call it into action, and that is *a gospel*, a message clear as light, which in its very essence is a force to quicken and stir the soul.

A starting-point for faith is the first necessity.

We look out upon the world and we see that some men have had such a gospel without being in any sense finished and systematic theologians. St. Paul and St. Peter and St. John had it. St. Chrysostom and St. Francis of Assisi and Savonarola had it. John Wesley and George Whitfield had it. In different ages and under different conditions these preachers had the primal message which moves men to believe. And in our own age, under our own conditions, a like message has been proclaimed with power. Père Lacordaire preached such a message in Notre Dâme, and Canon Liddon in

Preaching with power.

St. Paul's, to listening thousands. Bishop
Brooks made it thrill like a celestial music
through the young manhood of America; and
Dwight L. Moody has spoken it with vigorous
directness in every great city that knows the
English tongue. In many things, in ecclesiastical relation, in theological statement, in dress,
in manner, in language, these preachers are
unlike. One thing only is the same in all of
them, and that is the source of their power.
Their central message, the core of their preaching, is the piercing, moving, personal gospel
of Jesus of Nazareth, the Son of God and Sav
iour of mankind. This, in its simplest form ;
this, in its clearest expression ; this presentation of a person to persons in order that they
may first know, and then love and trust and
follow Him — this is pre-eminently the gospel
for an age of doubt.

I

*The Gospel
of Christ.*

The adaptation of our central message, thus
conceived and thus expressed, to meet the
peculiar needs of a time of general scepticism,
is the theme of this lecture. I do not say that
this is the whole of Christianity. I do not say
that when the preacher has delivered this message in this form he has fulfilled all of his

duties. He may have to bear testimony against errors of thought and vices of conduct; he is certainly bound to give encouragement and guidance to new efforts of virtue and new enterprises of benevolence in every field. But his first and greatest duty, the discharge of which is to give him influence over doubting hearts and strength for all his other work, is simply to preach Christ.

This gospel meets the needs of the present time because it is the gospel of a fact.

The gospel of a fact.

Personality is a fact. Indeed we may say that it is the aboriginal fact; the source of all perception; the starting-point of all thought; the informing and moulding principle of all language. "All human observation implies that the mind, the 'I,' is a thing in itself, a fixed point in a world of change, of which world of change its own organs form a part. It is the same, yesterday, to-day, and to-morrow. It was what it is, when its organs were of a different shape and consisted of different matter from their present shape and matter. It will be what it is, when they have gone through other changes." [1]

[1] Sir James Fitzjames Stephen, *Liberty, Equality, Fraternity*. Quoted by Hutton, *Contemporary Thought*, I., p. 114.

Personality is the foundation.

This fact of a rational, free, conscious, persist-ent self is the foundation of all sensation and of all reflection; it is the basis of physics as well as of metaphysics. By contrast it gives us our first notion of matter ; by resistance, our first notion of force ; by operation, our first notion of causality. It is a necessary assumption even in the philosophies of agnosticism, positivism, and materialism. They cannot move a step without it.

" They reckon ill who leave *me* out."

To deny personality is to deny the possibility of any kind of knowledge and reduce the uni-verse to a blank.[1]

Moreover, it is not only true that the recogni-tion of our own personality lies at the root of perception and reasoning. It is also true that contact with other personalities, conscious, in-telligent, free, and persistent like ourselves, is the gateway through which we reach the reality of all external things. To a solitary mind the outward world may be only a dream. But the moment two minds come into contact and com-munication, it becomes at least a permanent possibility of sensation. By comparison and contrast with the sensations and experiences of

[1] Alfred Williams Momerie, *Personality, the Beginning and End of Metaphysics* (Blackwood, 1889), pp. 23, 132.

others, we verify our own. If it were not for this the whole universe would dissolve around us like the baseless fabric of a vision. The subtle analysis of modern science, transforming the apparently solid elements into invisible atoms, and these atoms into vortex rings in the impalpable and immeasurable ether, throws us back, more and more, upon personality, subjective and objective, as the only thing that remains sure and immutable.

Persons, then, are the most real and substantial objects of our knowledge. They touch us at more points, they affect us in more ways and with greater intensity, they fit more closely into the faculties and powers of our own being, than anything else in the universe. A person who has influenced us or our fellow-men leaves a more profound, positive, permanent, and real impression than any other fact whatsoever. We live as persons in a world of persons, far more truly than we live in a world of phenomena or laws or ideas.

Persons are realities.

Now, in an age that is characterized, as some German writer has said, by "a hunger for facts," the gospel of a person, if it is rightly apprehended and preached, ought to have peculiar power because it is a factual gospel. We can come to those who are under the benumbing spell of universal doubt and say : Here is a fact, a personality, real and imperishable. It is not merely a doctrine that was believed in Palestine eighteen hundred years ago. It is some one who was born and lived among men. It is not merely a theory of God and the soul and the future life that sprang up in the East in the first century and has strangely spread itself over the world. This religion is historical in every sense of the word, as the actual fulfilment of an ancient hope, and the starting-point of a new life.

The reality of Christ.

The person of Jesus Christ stands solid in the history of man. He is indeed more substantial, more abiding, in human apprehension, than any form of matter, or any mode of force. The conceptions of earth and air and fire and water change and melt around Him, as the clouds melt and change around an everlasting mountain peak. All attempts to resolve Him into a myth, a legend, an idea, — and hundreds of such attempts have been made, — have drifted over the enduring reality of His character and left not a rack behind. The result of all criticism, the final verdict of enlightened commonsense, is that Christ is historical. He is such a person as men could not have imagined if they would, and would not have imagined if they could. He is neither Greek myth, nor Hebrew legend. The artist capable of fashioning Him did not exist, nor could he have found the materials. A non-existent Christianity did not spring out of the air and create a Christ. A real Christ appeared in the world and created Christianity. This is what we mean by the gospel of a fact.

II

And here we come at once into sight of the second quality of this gospel which is peculiarly fitted to meet the needs of a doubting age.

The gospel of a force.

If it be true that a person is a fact, it is no less true that a person is a force. The world moves by personality. All the great currents of history have flowed from persons. Organization is powerful; but no organization has ever accomplished anything until a person has stood at the centre of it and filled it with his thought, with his life. Truth is mighty and must prevail. But it never does prevail actually until it gets itself embodied, incarnated, in a personality. Christianity has an organization. Christianity has a doctrine. But the force of Christianity, that which made it move and lent it power to move the world, is the Person at the heart of it, who gives vitality to the organization and reality to the doctrine. All the abstract truths of Christianity might have come into the world in another form, — nay, the substance of these truths did actually come into the world, dimly and partially through the fragmentary religions of the nations, more clearly and with increasing, prophetic light through the inspired Scriptures of the Hebrews; but still the world would not stir, still the truth could not make itself felt as a universal force in the life of humanity until

> "The Word had breath, and wrought
> With human hands the creed of creeds,
> In loveliness of perfect deeds,
> More strong than all poetic thought." [1]

I think we must get back, in our conception of Christianity and in our preaching of it, to this primary position. The fount and origin of its power was, and continued to be, and still is, the Person Christ.

Christ was His own gospel.

This was the secret of His ministry. He Himself was the central word of His own preaching. He offered Himself to the world as the solution of its difficulties and the source

[1] Tennyson, *In Memoriam*, xxxvi.

of a new life. He asked men simply to believe in Him, to love Him, to follow Him. He
called the self-righteous to humble themselves
to His correction, the sinful to confide in His
forgiveness, the doubting to trust His assurance, and the believing to accept His guidance into fuller light.[1] To those who became
His disciples He gave doctrine and instruction
in many things. But to those who were not
yet His disciples, to the world, He offered first
of all Himself, not a doctrine, not a plan of
life, but a living Person. This was the substance of His first sermon when He stood up
in the synagogue at Nazareth and having read
from the Book of Isaiah the prophecy of the
Great Liberator, declared unto the people
"This day is this Scripture fulfilled in your
ears."[2] This was the attraction of His universal invitation, "Come unto Me, all ye that
labour and are heavy laden and I will give
you rest."[3] This was the heart of His summary of His completed work when He said, "I,
if I be lifted up from the earth, will draw all
men unto Me."[4]

[1] Henry Latham, *Pastor Pastorum* (New York, James
Pott & Co., 1891), pp. 273–275.

[2] St. Luke iv. 16–21.

[3] St. Matt. xi. 28.

[4] St. John xii. 32.

We are not considering, at this moment, the tremendous implications of such a personal self-assertion, unparalleled, I believe, in the founder of any other religion. We pass by for the present that famous and inevitable alternative, *Aut Christus Deus, aut homo non bonus est.* The point, now, is simply this. As a matter of history, setting aside all question of the divine inspiration and authority of the Gospels, taking them merely as a trustworthy report of a certain sequence of events,[1] it is plain that the force which started the religion of Jesus was the person Jesus. Christ was His own Christianity. Christ was the core of His own gospel.

The life of the Church flowed from Christ.

Read on through the other books of the New Testament, the Acts and the Epistles, and you will see that they are just the record of the operation of this force in life and literature. It was this that sent the apostles out into the

---

[1] The evidence for the historic trustworthiness of the Gospels may be found summed up in its modern form in Dr. Salmon's *Introduction to the New Testament*, fourth edition (New York, Young & Co., 1889); in Bishop Lightfoot's *Essays on "Supernatural Religion"* (Macmillan, 1889); in Beyschlag's *New Testament Theology* (Edinburgh, T. & T. Clark, 1895), pp. 29–31, 216–221 of volume i.; and in Prof. George P. Fisher's *Grounds of Theistic and Christian Belief* (Scribners, 1883).

world, reluctantly and hesitatingly at first, then
joyfully and triumphantly, like men driven by
an irresistible impulse. It was the manifestation of Christ that converted them,[1] the love
of Christ that constrained them,[2] the power of
Christ that impelled them.[3] He was their
certainty[4] and their strength.[5] He was their
peace[6] and their hope.[7] For Christ they la-
boured and suffered ;[8] in Christ they gloried ;[9]
for Christ's sake they lived and died.[10] They
felt and they declared that the life that was in
them was His life.[11] They were confident that
they could do all things through Christ which
strengthened them.[12] The offices of the Church
— apostle, bishop, deacon, evangelist, — call
them by what names you will — were simply
forms of service to Him as Master ;[13] the
doctrines of the Church were simply unfoldings of what she had received from Him as
Teacher ;[14] the worship of the Church, as distinguished from that of the Jewish Synagogue
and the Heathen Temple, was the adoration
of Christ as Lord.[15]

Now it was precisely this relation of the

[1] Gal. i. 16. [6] Eph. ii. 14. [11] Gal. ii. 20.
[2] 2 Cor. v. 14. [7] Col. i. 27. [12] Phil. iv. 13.
[3] 2 Cor. xii. 9. [8] Phil. iii. 8–10. [13] Eph. iv. 8–12.
[4] 2 Tim. i. 12. [9] Gal. vi. 14. [14] 1 Cor. xi. 1, 23 ; xv. 3.
[5] 2 Tim. ii. 1. [10] 2 Cor. iv. 5, 11. [15] Phil. ii. 11; 1 Cor. xii. 3.

*The influ-
ence of
Christianity
came from
Christ.*

early Church, in her organization and doctrine and worship, to the person Christ, held fast in her memory as identical with the real Jesus who was born in Bethlehem and crucified on Calvary, conceived in her faith as still living and present with His disciples, — it was this personal animation of the Church by Christ that gave her influence over men. Contrary to all human probability, against the prejudice of the Hebrews who abhorred the name of a crucified man, against the prejudice of the Greeks and Romans who despised the name of a common Jew, she made her way, not by concealing, but by exalting and glorifying, the name of Jesus Christ. Indeed, it seems as if her career of conquest was actually delayed until that name was taken up and written upon her banners. It was in Antioch, where the disciples were first called Christians,[1] that the missionary enterprise of the Church began, and it was from that centre, with that title, that she went out to her triumph.

*The magic
of Christ's
name.*

The name of Christ was magical; not as a secret and unintelligible incantation, but as the sign of a real person, known and loved. It enlightened and healed and quickened the heart of an age which, like our own, was dark

---

[1] Acts xi. 26; xiii. 1–3.

and sorrowful and heavy with doubt. It was
the charm which drew men to Christianity out
of the abstractions of philosophy,[1] and the confusions of idolatry darkened with a thousand
personifications but empty of all true personality. The music of that name rang through
all the temple of the Church, and to its harmonies her walls were builded. The acknowledgment of that name was the mark of Christian
discipleship. To confess that "Jesus is the
Christ" was the way to enter the Church. The
symbolism of that name was the mark of Christian worship. The central rites of the Church
were baptism into Christ and communion with
Christ. Fidelity to His name was the crown
of Christian martyrdom. Unnumbered multitudes of men and women and children went
down to death because they would not deny
the Christ. Whatever the early Church
was and did, beyond a doubt her character
and her activity were but the resultant of
the personal influence that flowed from Jesus
Christ.[2]

When we turn to follow the history of Christianity through the later centuries down to the

---

[1] See Justin Martyr, *Dialogue with Trypho*, chap. viii.

[2] George B. Stevens, *The Pauline Theology* (New York,
Scribners, 1892), pp. 321–323.

F

The personal power of Christ continues.

present time, we see that the same thing is true. The temporal power of the Bishop of Rome doubtless grew out of the union of the Church with the Empire. The immense wealth and secular authority of ecclesiastics may be traced to social and political causes. But the inward, vitalizing, self-propagating power of Christianity as a religion has always come from the person of Jesus who stands at the heart of

Christ is the charm of Christianity.

it. The attraction of its hymns and psalms and spiritual songs, the beauty of its holy days and solemn ceremonies, were derived from Him who is the central figure in praise and prayer. The renaissance of Christian Art sprang from the desire to picture to the imagination the visible, adorable form and face of Him whom speculative theology had so often concealed or obscured. The penetrating and abiding fragrance of Christian literature resides in those books, like *The Imitation of Christ*, in which the sweetness of His character is embalmed forever. The potency of Christian preaching comes from, and is measured by, the clearness of the light which it throws upon the personality of Jesus. Read the roll of those in every age whom the world has acknowledged as the best Christians, kings and warriors and philosophers, martyrs and heroes and labourers in every noble cause, the purest and the highest of mankind, and you will see that the test by which they are judged, the mark by which they are recognized, is likeness and loyalty to the personal Christ. Then turn to the work which the Church is doing to-day in the lowest and darkest fields of human life, among the submerged classes of our great cities, among the sunken races of heathendom, and you cannot deny that the force of that work to enlighten and uplift, still depends upon the simplicity and reality with which it reveals the person of Jesus to the hearts of men. Christianity as a missionary religion would be fatally crippled if you took out of it the familiar story of Jesus and His love.

"Mr. Darwin," says Admiral Sir James Sullivan, "had often expressed to me his conviction that it was utterly useless to send missionaries to such a set of savages as the Fuegians, probably the very lowest of the human race. I had always replied that I did not believe any human beings existed too low to comprehend the simple message of the Gospel of Christ. After many years he wrote to me that the recent account of the mission showed that he had been wrong and I right . . . and he requested me to forward to the Society an enclosed cheque

The testimony of a doubter.

for £5, as a testimony of his interest in their good work." [1]

The force which breaks the inertia of unbelief.

Observe, we are not constructing an argument. We are only tracing a force, — the force that flows from the person of Jesus Christ. The more closely, the more powerfully we can feel it in ourselves and in others, the more confidently we can come to a doubting age and say : Here is this force, intense, persistent, far-reaching. It has moved all kinds of men, from the highest to the lowest. What do you make of it ? What will you do with it ? Is it not the only thing that can lift and move you out of your doubt ? For scepticism is just the inertia of the soul which stands poised between contrary and mutually destructive theories. From that state of impotence there is but one deliverance, and that is by force, the force of life embodied in a person.

III

The gospel of a real spiritual world.

But the force which proceeds from the person of Jesus is not mere power, blind and purposeless. It moves always in a certain direction. It has a quality in it which produces certain

[1] Alfred Barry, *Some Lights of Science on the Faith* (London, Longmans, 1892), p. 116.

results. And one of these results is an immediate and overwhelming sense of the reality and nearness of spiritual things. This is the third point of adaptation in the gospel of the personal Christ to the needs of a sceptical age. It carries with itself an evidence of things not seen, a substance of things hoped for.

An aura of wonder and mystery surrounded *The mystery of Jesus.* Jesus of Nazareth in His earthly life. All who came in contact with Him felt it; in love, if they desired to believe; in repulsion, if they hated to believe. In His presence, faith in the invisible, in the soul, in the future life, in God, revived and unfolded with new bloom and colour. In His presence hypocrisy was silenced and afraid, but sincere piety found a voice and prayed. This effluence of His character breathes from the whole record of His life. It was not merely what He said to men about the eternal verities that convinced them. It was something in Himself, an atmosphere surrounding Him, and a silent radiance shining from Him, that made it easier for them to believe in their own spiritual nature and in the Divine existence and presence. He drew out of their fallen and neglected hearts, by some celestial attraction, spontaneous, gentle, irresistible, a new efflorescence of faith and hope and love. Where He came a spiritual springtide flowed over the landscape of the inner life. Blossoms appeared in the earth and the time for the singing of birds was come.

Faith was not imposed on doubting hearts by an external and mechanical process. It grew in the warmth that streamed from Him. It was not merely that men were at their best in His company, except, indeed, those who were at their worst through sullen resistance and malignant alarm at His power. It was that men were conscious of something far better than their best, a transcendent force, an influence from the immeasurable heights above them. And to withstand it they must sink below themselves, make new falsehoods and new negations to bind them down, grapple themselves more closely to the base, the earthly, the sensual. But if they yielded to that influence, it lifted and moved their thoughts inevitably upward. It was not merely what He told them of His own sight of spiritual things. It was what they saw reflected in His face and form of that loftier, wider outlook. He was like one standing on a high peak, reporting of the sunrise to men in the dark valley. They heard His words. But they saw also upon His countenance the glow of dawn, and dazzling all about Him the incommunicable splendours of a new day.

This was the effect of the personality of Jesus, as He stood amid the shadows and uncertainties of human life; an effect strangely overlooked and ignored, often even beclouded and hidden, in much that has been written about Him by theologians and historians. I do not dream that I can put it into words. But I know that it can be felt as a reality in the Gospels. And I turn back to one who saw Him face to face, one who touched His hand and leaned upon His bosom, for the expression of the soul-uplifting, faith-begetting wonder of the person of Christ : *The Word was made flesh and dwelt among us, and we beheld His glory, the glory as of the only-begotten of the Father, full of grace and truth.*[1]

Nor has this effect vanished from the world with the removal of the bodily presence of Jesus. It has perpetuated itself by its own vital power, increasing rather than diminishing. It still flows from the picture of His life which is preserved in the Gospels, from the image of His character as it is formed in the minds of men. Eliminate, if you please, what is called the miraculous element. Make what

The influence of His picture.

[1] St. John i. 14.

allowance you will for the enthusiasm and unguarded utterance of His disciples. There still remains that enthusiasm itself to be reckoned with, an enthusiasm which was kindled by Him alone. There still remains the figure of the person of Christ, who never can be expressed in terms of matter and force, who never can be explained by natural and historical causes, who carries us by His own inherent mystery into the presence of the spiritual, the divine, the supernatural.

Christ unique.

Something of this spiritual light, I will admit, — nay, I will maintain with joyous and firm conviction, — comes from every human personality, even the lowliest, in so far as it refuses to be summed up in terms of sense perception, in so far as it gives evidence, by its affections and hopes and fears, of elements in man that are not of the dust. But in Christ this light is transcendent and unique, because He manifestly surpasses the ordinary attainments of humanity, because He cannot be accounted for by the laws of heredity and environment. The more closely we apply these laws, the more clearly He shines out above them.[1]

"The learned men of our day," says M.

[1] J. S. Mill, *Essays on Religion*, p. 253.

Pierre Loti in his latest book, *La Galilée*, "have endeavoured to find a human explication of His mission, but they have not yet reached it. . . . Around Him, none the less, there still glows a radiance of beams which cannot be comprehended."[1]

Historically He appears alone, as no great man has ever appeared before or since. Heroes, teachers, and leaders of men have always been seen as central stars in larger constellations, surrounded by lesser but kindred lights. Plato shines in conjunction with Socrates and Aristotle; Cæsar with Pompey and Crassus; Luther with Melanchthon and Calvin; Shakespeare with Beaumont and Fletcher and Ben Jonson; Napoleon surrounded with his brilliant staff of marshals and diplomats; Wordsworth among the mild glories of the Lake poets. In every case, if you search the neighbourhood of a great name, you will find not a blank sky, but an encircling galaxy. But Jesus Christ stands in an immense solitude. Among the prophets who predicted Him, among the apostles who testified of Him, there is none worthy to be compared or conjoined with Him. It is as if the heavens were swept bare of stars; and suddenly, un-

Christ solitary.

[1] Pierre Loti, *La Galilée* (Paris, 1895), p. 93.

expected, unaccompanied, the light of lights appears alone, in supreme isolation.

Nor is there anything in His antecedents, in His surroundings, to explain His appearance and radiance. There was nothing in the soil of the sordid and narrow Jewish race to produce such an embodiment of pure and universal love.[1] There was nothing in the atmosphere of that corrupt and sensual age to beget or foster such a character of stainless and complete virtue. Nor was His own life, — I say it reverently, — judged by purely human and natural laws, calculated to result in such an evident perfection as all men have wonderingly recognized in Him. The highest type of human piety, the excellence of a beautiful soul, has never been reached among men without repentance and self-abasement. But Jesus never repented, never abased Himself in shame and sorrow before God, never asked for pardon and mercy. Alone, among His followers who kneel at His command to confess their unworthiness and implore forgiveness, He stands upright and lifts a cloudless face to heaven in the inexplicable glory

[1] Amory H. Bradford, *Heredity and Christian Problems* (New York, Macmillan, 1895), p. 266.

of piety without penitence. Moral perfection of this kind is not only without a parallel; it is also without an approach. Men have never attained to it, and there is no way for them to climb thither. We can only look up to that perfection, serene, sinless, unsurpassable, and feel that here we are in sight of something which cannot be expressed except by saying that it is the glory of eternal spirit embodied in a person.

IV

But the force which resides in the person of Jesus is not exhausted in the production of this profound impression of its own spiritual and transcendent nature. It goes beyond this result of a vivid sense of the reality of the unseen. It has in itself a purifying, cleansing power, a delivering, uplifting, sanctifying power. The Gospel of Christ is the gospel of a person who saves men from sin. And herein it comes very close to the heart of a doubting age.

The gospel of a Saviour.

The great and wonderful fact of this experience, which can neither be questioned nor fully explained, is not involved in the theological speculations which have gathered about

it. The person of Jesus stands out clear
and simple as a powerful Saviour of sinful
men and women. In His presence, the publican and the harlot felt their hearts dissolve
with I know not what unutterable rapture
of forgiveness. At His word, the heavy-
laden were mysteriously loosed from the
imponderable burden of past transgression.
He suffered with sinners, and even while
He suffered He delivered them from the
sharpest of all pains, — the pain of conscious

*The power
of Christ's
cross.*

and unpardoned evil. He died for sinners,
according to His own word ; and ever since,
His cross has been the sign of rescue for
humanity. Whatever may be the nature
of that sublime transaction upon Calvary;
whatever the name by which men call it, —
Atonement, Sacrifice, Redemption, Propitia-
tion ; whatever relations it may have to the
eternal moral law and to the Divine righteousness, — its relation to the human heart is
luminous and beautiful. It does take away
sin. Kneeling at that holy altar, the soul at
once remembers most vividly, and confesses
most humbly, and loses most entirely, all her
guilt. A sense of profound, unutterable relief,
a sacred quietude, diffuses itself through all
the recesses of the troubled spirit. Looking

unto Christ crucified, we receive an assurance
of sin forgiven, which goes deeper than thought
can fathom, and far deeper than words can
measure.

> " We may not know, we cannot tell
>   What pains He had to bear,
> But we believe it was for us
>   He hung and suffered there.
>
> " He died that we might be forgiven,
>   He died to make us good ;
> That we might go at last to heaven,
>   Saved by His precious blood."

This is not theory, this is not philosophy,
this is not theology. It is veritable fact. The
person Jesus, living with men, dying for men,
has actually brought this gift of pardon for
the past and hope for the future, into the heart
of mankind. And from pure love of Him — a
love which is first of all and most of all a sense
of gratitude for this immeasurable service —
have blossomed, often out of the very abysses of
sin and degradation, the saintliest and sublimest
lives that the world has ever seen.

Now this, as I know from my own experience,
is the gospel for doubting men, and for an age
of doubt ; the gospel of a Person who is a fact

and a force, an evidence of the unseen, and a
Saviour from sin. Can we preach it? Will we
preach it? Then one thing is necessary for
us, a thing which might not be necessary,
perhaps, if our message were of another kind.

All knowledge, of the world, of human nature, of books, will be helpful and tributary;
all gifts, of clear thought, of powerful speech,
of prudent action, will be valuable and should
be cultivated; but one thing will be absolutely and forever indispensable.

To know Christ, the one thing need-ful.

If we are to preach Christ we must know
Christ, and know Him in such a sense that we
can say with St. Paul that we are determined
not to know anything save Jesus Christ and
Him crucified.[1] We must study Him in the
record of His life until His character is more
real and vivid to us than that of brother or
friend. We must imagine Him with ardent
soul, until His figure glows before our inward
sight, and His words sound in our ears as a
living voice. We must love with His love, and
sorrow with His grief, and rejoice with His joy,
and offer ourselves with His sacrifice, so truly,
so intensely that we can say, as St. Paul said,
that we are crucified by His cross and risen in
His resurrection.[2] We must trace the power

[1] 1 Cor. ii. 2.   [2] Gal. ii. 20.

of His life in the lives of our fellow-men, following and realizing His triumphs in souls redeemed and sins forgiven, until we know the rapture that thrilled the breast of a St. Bernard, a St. Francis, a Thomas à Kempis, a Samuel Rutherford, a Robert McCheyne ; the chivalrous loyalty that animated a Henry Havelock, a Charles Kingsley, a Frederick Robertson, a Charles Gordon ; the deep devotion that strengthened a David Brainerd, a Henry Martyn, a Coleridge Patteson. We must become the brothers of these men through brotherhood with Christ. We must kindle our hearts in communion with Him, by meditation, by prayer, and by service, which is the best kind of prayer. No day must pass in which we do not do something distinctly in Jesus' name, for Jesus' sake. We must go where He would go if He were on earth. We must try to do what He would do if He were still among men. And so, by our failure as well as by our effort, by the very contrast between our incompleteness and His perfection, the image of our Companion and our saving Lord will grow radiant and distinct within us. We shall know that potent attraction which His person has exercised upon the hearts of men, and feel in our breast that overmastering sense of loyalty

to Him, which alone can draw us to follow
Him through life and death.

> "If Jesus Christ is a man, —
>   And only a man, — I say
> That of all mankind I cleave to Him,
>   And to Him will I cleave alway.

> "If Jesus Christ is a God, —
>   And the only God, — I swear
> I will follow Him through heaven and hell,
>   The earth, the sea, and the air." [1]

[1] Richard Watson Gilder, "Song of a Heathen, sojourning
in Galilee, A.D. 32."

III

THE UNVEILING OF THE FATHER

" He, who from the Father forth was sent,
   Came the true Light, light to our hearts to bring;
   The Word of God, — the telling of His thought;
   The Light of God, — the making visible;
   The far-transcending glory brought
   In human form with man to dwell;
   The dazzling gone — the power not less
   To show, irradiate, and bless;
   The gathering of the primal rays divine,
   Informing Chaos to a pure sunshine!"

—GEORGE MACDONALD.

III

THE UNVEILING OF THE FATHER

IN the famous fifteenth chapter of *The De-cline and Fall of the Roman Empire*, the author, who was but a superficial sceptic though a profound historian, introduces an account of the rise and spread of the Christian Religion. He attributes its remarkable triumph over the established religions of the earth to a series of causes which he ironically describes as secondary, and uniformly treats as primary. He exhibits them as in themselves sufficient to explain the peculiarly favourable reception of the Christian faith in the world, and sets aside the question of a possible divine origin as unnecessary. With serene self-satisfaction he traces the rapid growth of the Christian Church to the five following causes: I. *The Zeal of the Christians*, derived from the Jews, — but purified from that narrow and unsocial spirit which, instead of inviting, had deterred the Gentiles from embracing the law of Moses.

A sceptic's account of the spread of Christianity.

83

II. *The Doctrine of a Future Life*, improved by every additional circumstance which could give weight and efficacy to that important truth. III. *The Miraculous Powers* ascribed to the primitive Church. IV. *The Pure and Austere Morals* of the Christians. V. *The Union and Discipline of the Christian Republic*, which gradually formed an increasing and independent state in the heart of the Roman empire.[1]

The shallowness of this view.

Now this is a very fair, we may even say a brilliant, example of the kind of work which was done by the shallow and complacent scepticism of a century ago. But the moment we subject it to the more searching analysis of the scepticism of the present age, it dissolves into a thin and incoherent absurdity. For it is evident that, so far from giving an explanation of the growth of Christianity, Gibbon is simply describing some of the phenomena which accompanied that growth. What, for example, is " the zeal of the Christians " but an unilluminating name for a contagious and irresistible enthusiasm which spread through the world in connection with faith in Christ ? What is

[1] Edward Gibbon, Esq., *A History of the Decline and Fall of the Roman Empire* (London, John Murray, 8th Edition, 1854), vol. ii., p. 152.

" the union and discipline of the Christian republic " but a description, without explanation,
of the organic unfolding of a new, mysterious principle of fellowship. These alleged
" causes," more closely examined, are in fact
the very things that require to be accounted
for. Instead of clearing up the mystery, they
increase it.

By a singular fatality of language, the sceptical historian has embodied in the statement
of his position the demonstration of its insufficiency. In each of his causes, and in the
relation that subsists between them, he has
practically suggested a difficulty which demands another and a higher solution of the
whole problem. Examine his words carefully.

The " ex-
planation "
needs to be
explained.

By what means, human or divine, was the
zeal of the Christians ' purified from the narrow
and unsocial spirit of the Jews ' ? The natural
history of sects and schisms teaches us that
their invariable tendency is to intensify rather
than to eliminate bigotry and exclusiveness.
Through what influence was the doctrine of a
future life ' improved by every additional circumstance that could give it weight and efficacy ' ? The inevitable course of its human
development under the guidance of abstract
philosophy has been towards vagueness, cold-

Questions
which de-
mand an
answer.

ness, and uncertainty; under the guidance of concrete superstition, towards puerility and crass sensualism. On what grounds were miraculous powers ascribed to the early Church? They must have been ascribed truly or falsely. If truly, there must have been some basis of fact for them to rest upon. If falsely, the Christians themselves were either ignorant, or cognizant, of the falsehood. Take the former supposition, and you present yourself with the inexplicable theory that what Pliny the Younger called *superstitio prava immodica*, and imagined would be easily and certainly extirpated, was able to hold its own against all the assaults of learning and philosophy. Take the latter supposition, and you are forced to the incredible assumption that a conscious deception was the fountain of highest and strongest moral force that the world has ever felt.[1] How then did the "pure and austere morals of the Christians" come into existence? From a lie, or from a truth? If from a truth, what was the nature of that truth, in what form was it expressed, and how did it win credence?

[1] Carlyle, *Heroes and Hero-Worship*, sect. ii.: "A false man found a religion? Why, a false man cannot even build a brick house! If he do not know and follow *truly* the properties of mortar, burnt clay, and what else he works in, it is no house that he makes, but a rubbish heap."

And, finally, how did "the Christian republic" succeed in maintaining and increasing itself as an independent state in the heart of the Roman empire? Every other attempt to do this particular thing, by secret philosophic doctrine, or by open political organization, failed, and was violently crushed by imperial power, or silently dissolved and absorbed by imperial statesmanship. How was it that this one invisible fellowship, this one visible organization, lived, and spread, and stood out at last, serene, complete, and magnificent, when the time-worn ruins of the empire crumbled around it?

The answer to these questions is found in the person of Christ. This is not a matter of choice. It is a matter of necessity. For if He was, as all candid observers will admit, the originator and animator of Christianity, then to stop short of Him in our inquiry as to the causes of its existence and progress is to stop half-way, as if one should account for the flow of the Nile, after the fashion of the ancient geographers, by attributing it to the melting of the snows on the Mountains of the Moon, instead of tracing it to its great fountain in the Albert Nyanza.

Christ stands above and behind the Church, and all these secondary causes which have been

The answer is Christ.

enumerated to account for her growth and power flow directly from Him. He it was who purified and humanized the zeal of Christians, so that they emerged from the narrowest of races to preach the broadest and most universal of all religions. He it was who cleared and enlarged their view of immortality, so that it became at once important and efficacious, the only doctrine of a future life that has exercised a direct and uplifting influence upon the present life. He it was who endowed the Church with whatever powers she possessed. He it was who cleansed and ennobled her moral ideals and gave her the only pattern and rule of virtue which has been universally acknowledged as self-consistent, satisfactory, and supreme. He it was who cemented her union and strengthened her discipline to such an indestructible solidarity, that the tie which bound the individual soul to Him was regarded as superior to all earthly relations, and the fellowship which that common tie created, surpassed and survived all fellowships of race, of culture, of nationality.

These are simple historical facts. In stating them we make no assumptions and propound no theories. It is not necessary to take anything for granted or to adopt any particular theological or philosophical system, in order to see clearly and beyond the possibility of mistake that all the force and influence of Christianity in the world have, as a matter of fact, flowed directly from Jesus Christ and from the faith which He has inspired in the hearts of men.

The one question of supreme importance, then, if we would understand what Christianity really means, is, Who is this person who stands at the centre of it and fills it with life and strength? What did the first Christians see in Him that made them believe in Him so absolutely and implicitly and gave them power to do such mighty works? What has the church seen in Him through the ages that has bound her to Him as her living Lord and Master? And what are we to see in Him if He is to be in deed and in truth the theme of our gospel? *What think ye of Christ?*

Who, then, is Christ?

This question, you see, is vital and inevitable. If we are to have a Christianity which is real and historical, we must get into line with history. If we are to have behind us the power which comes from actual achievements of our gospel in the world, we must understand the relation which it has always held to the person of Christ. If we are to be in any sense the followers of the first Christians, and to share the joy and peace and power of their religion, we

The inevitable question.

must take the view which they took, of Jesus of Nazareth.

The historic answer.

Now, the object of this lecture may be stated in a single sentence. It is to show that the first Christians saw, and that the Church has always seen, in Jesus Christ a real incarnation of God ; a true and personal unveiling of the Father ; God in Christ, reconciling the world unto Himself. In other words, not only must we find in Jesus Christ the centre of Christianity, but we must also behold an actual divinity as the centre of life in Jesus Christ.

I

Christ's Godhood slowly revealed.

We are not to suppose that faith in Christ began with a clear and definite conception of His divinity. On the contrary, it is evident from the whole gospel record that the idea that Christ was divine gradually developed and unfolded in the minds of those who knew and loved and trusted Him. The idea of an incarnation was foreign to the Hebrew mind. There was no race in the world that held so strongly to the thought that God was solitary, unsearchable, and incommunicable. They believed that even His true name could not be pronounced by human lips, and that it was impossible for human eyes really to behold His glory. And the very strength of this ancestral faith of theirs, standing as it must have done directly in the way of belief in an incarnation, is an evidence of the tremendous power and unquestionable reality of the experience which forced the disciples, by slow degrees, to believe firmly and unhesitatingly in the divinity of Christ.

The process by which this result was accomplished lies open to our thought in the New Testament. We must go back to the point indicated in the second lecture. It was the impression made upon the disciples by Christ's own manifestation of Himself, His character, His actions, and His words, evidently consistent and unique, which led them at last to see in Him the object of divine faith and worship. He was not a mere man. That was evident and undeniable. He was higher than men ; holier than men ; He possessed an excellence and a power which made them feel in His presence that He was more than they were. What then was He? There were but two directions in which their faith could move. The alternative was sharply set before the disciples on that memorable day at Cæsarea Philippi, when Christ asked them first, "Whom do men say that I, the Son of man, am ?" and then, "But whom say ye

The gradual process of faith.

that I am?" There were but two lines open to
them.   One was the line of popular superstition,
which led them back into the past to see in
Christ only the ghost of John the Baptist, or
Elias, or one of the prophets come to life again.
The other was the new line of Christian faith
which led them forward to see in Jesus "the
Christ, the Son of the living God." [1]

*The new
line of Chris-
tian belief.*

New?   Of course it was new !   It had to be
new, in order to fit the facts, which were such
as had never been seen before.   And just because it was so new it had to unfold itself by
degrees to the fulness of conscious apprehension
of all that it involved.

*What it
meant to be
the Christ.*

It is evident that the disciples did not know
at first what was meant by the Christhood,
the Messiahship, the fulfilment of all ancient
prophecy and sacred ritual in Jesus.   But they
learned the lesson as they kept company with
Him.   They heard Him speak with an authority which none of the prophets had ever claimed.
Recognizing a divine inspiration in the Old
Testament Scriptures, He distinctly set Himself above them as the bringer of a new and
better revelation.   He accomplished, interpreted,
and revised them.   " Ye have heard how it hath
been said by them of old time " — by whom?

[1] St. Matt. xvi. 13–16.

By the lawgivers and prophets and psalmists whom Christ recognized as His own forerunners and foretellers. "But I say unto you, love your enemies, bless them that curse you, and pray for them that despitefully use you." [1]

Suppose that this were all; suppose that the Sermon on the Mount were the whole of the New Testament, what should we behold in it? Not merely the amazing revelation of a morality more pure and perfect than any other the human heart has conceived, proceeding from the lips of an unlearned Nazarene peasant of the first century, but the absolutely overwhelming sight of a believing Hebrew placing Himself above the rule of His own faith, a humble teacher asserting supreme authority over all human conduct, a moral reformer discarding all other foundations, and saying, "Every one that heareth these sayings of mine and doeth them, I will liken him unto a wise man which built his house upon a rock." [2] Nine and forty times, in the brief and fragmentary record of the discourses of Jesus, recurs this solemn phrase with which He authenticates the truth: *Verily, I say unto you.* And every time that the disciples heard it they must have gotten a new idea of what it meant to be the Christ.

A new power to reveal truth.

[1] St. Matt. v. 43, 44. [2] St. Matt. vii. 24.

Think also of the significance which the favourite Messianic title used by Jesus to describe Himself must have had to their minds. He called Himself "the Son of man."[1] Why? Was it because He was merely human? If that was all, surely it would not need to be asserted and emphasized again and again. Imagine any other man, the highest and the holiest, insisting upon the reality of his human life, dwelling upon it, repeating the assertion of it over and over. But this title was, in fact, the claim to a peculiar and supreme relation to the human race. Christ was not *a* son of man, but *the* Son of man, one who, in the luminous words of Irenæus, *recapitulavit in se ipso longam hominum expositionem.*[2] And as such He assumed on earth and in His prevision of heaven a position which no mere man could rightly take. "The Son of man hath power on earth to forgive sins."[3] "The Son of man is Lord also of the Sabbath."[4] "When the Son of man shall come in His glory, and all the holy

---

[1] In St. Matthew, 30 times; in St. Luke, 25 times; in St. Mark, 14 times.

[2] Irenæus, *Adv. Hær.*, iii. 18. 1 : "He summed up in himself the long unfolding of humanity." The Syriac version of this passage is equally beautiful and significant: "He *commenced afresh* the long line of men."

[3] St. Matt. ix. 6.   [4] St. Mark ii. 28.

angels with Him, then shall He sit upon the throne of His glory ; and before Him shall be gathered all nations, and He shall separate them one from another, as a shepherd divideth the sheep from the goats." [1]

Consider what this implied. It was a decla- *A supreme* ration that Jesus expected, and was willing, to *authority to* take into His own hands the task of discrimi- *judge the* nating between the good and the bad in the *world.* unsearchable confusions and complexities of the human heart, and of determining, without hesitation, without misgiving, without redress, the final destinies of the untold myriads of men ; "an office," it has been well said, "involving such spiritual insight, such discernment of the thoughts and intents of the heart of each one of the millions at His feet, such awful, unshared supremacy in the moral world, that the imagination recoils in sheer agony from the task of seriously contemplating the assumption of these duties by any created intelligence." [2] When the disciples heard their Master declare that He would fulfil this office of Judge of the World, they must have begun to feel what it meant to be the Christ.

[1] St. Matt. xxv. 31, 32.
[2] H. P. Liddon, *The Divinity of Our Lord* (London, 1885), p. 176.

What it meant to be the Son of God.

Nor do I suppose that they realized at first the full intention of that second phrase in which their view of Jesus was expressed. *The Son of the living God*, — that also was an idea to be gradually apprehended and unfolded. And think what light must have fallen upon it from the conduct of Jesus as they followed Him from day to day. The more closely they knew Him, the more deeply they felt His sinless purity and sovereign virtue. There was a certainty, an independence, a freedom from all effort and from all restraint in His goodness, such as no other good man has ever shown. He had the deepest knowledge of the evil of sin, yet no shadow or stain of it fell upon His own soul. He was on terms of closest intimacy — an intimacy such as no saint ever dared to assume — with God. He conversed with the Father in a friendship which was utterly without fear or regret or misgiving.

Christ's own words.

Now when the disciples saw this, it must have put them upon deep thoughts, and the guidance to these thoughts was given by Christ's own words about Himself. He put Himself side by side with the Divine activity. "My Father worketh hitherto and I work." [1] The Jews who heard Him say this, sought to kill Him,

[1] St. John v. 17.

because He had not only broken the Sabbath, but said also that God was His Father, making Himself equal with God. And if the Jews thought this, what did His own disciples think? He claimed a Divine origin and mission : " I came forth from the Father ; "[1] " My Father sent me."[2] He claimed a Divine knowledge and fellowship : " No man knoweth the Father save the Son ; "[3] " O righteous Father, the world hath not known Thee, but I have known Thee."[4] He claimed to unveil the Father's being in Himself : " He that hath seen me hath seen the Father. I am in the Father and the Father in me."[5]

To what conclusion must such conduct and such words as these lead the disciples in their interpretation of the true meaning of the title "the Son of God"? A conclusion which Jesus Himself, if He was as wise and good as all men admit, must inevitably have foreseen. A conclusion which He Himself, if He had been only a holy man, better than His disciples but of the same nature, would certainly have guarded against and prevented at any cost. A conclusion which is expressed in the attitude of

The inevitable conclusion

---

[1] St. John xvi. 28. [3] St. Matt. xi. 27.
[2] St. John xii. 49. [4] St. John xvii. 25.
[5] St. John xiv. 9, 11.

H

Thomas, kneeling at the feet of Christ and crying, " My Lord and my God." [1]   A conclusion which is finally and definitively embodied in the action of the apostles going out into the world to disciple all nations, and to baptize them " into the name of the Father, and of the Son, and of the Holy Ghost." [2]

II

The disciples believed that Christ was Divine.

There cannot be any question as to the state of mind which this action implied.   It was the deep conviction, not necessarily reasoned out and formulated, but lying at the very root of conduct, that Jesus Christ the Son was the unveiling of His Father God, and that the Holy Spirit who came upon the disciples was the Spirit of the Father and the Son.   The part which the resurrection played in the clarifying and confirming of this conviction was important.   But we must not misunderstand the meaning of the resurrection.   It was not in any sense a new and different revelation of God, imagined or actually received.   Whatever the form in which Jesus appeared to the disciples during the forty days that followed His death, He was recognized as the same Jesus ; and the one effect of His appearance was

[1] St. John xx. 28.   [2] St. Matt. xxviii. 19.

simply to confirm and deepen the truth of what
He had said and done while He was with them.
And with this confirmation the truth took shape
and substance as an active and enduring power
in human faith and life and worship.

There is no more room for doubt that the
early Christians saw in Christ a personal unveiling of God, than that the friends and followers of Abraham Lincoln regarded him as a
good and loyal American citizen of the white
race. And even if we could find no direct and
definite statement of either of these views, the
evidence that men held them could be clearly
and certainly read in the facts of history.

Divine honours were paid to Christ in the *The early*
primitive Church. The first common prayer *Church*
of the disciples, when they were assembled to *worshipped*
choose an apostle in the place of the traitor *Christ.*
Judas, was addressed to Christ.[1] The Christians were distinguished both from the Jews
and from the heathen as those who called upon
the name of the Lord Jesus Christ.[2] The dying
martyr Stephen showed what was meant by this
phrase in his prayer, " Lord Jesus, receive my
spirit."[3] Saul of Tarsus, when he was con-

[1] Acts i. 24. See Alford *in loc.*
[2] Acts ix. 21 ; 1 Cor. i. 2.
[3] Acts vii. 59.

vinced by that strange experience on the road
to Damascus that Jesus was not an impostor,
but the Christ, at once addressed Him in
prayer, "Lord, what wilt thou have me to
do?" [1]   And Ananias, who received Saul into
the Church, asked guidance and direction from
the same Lord. [2]   Peter baptized the multitudes on the day of Pentecost in the name of
Jesus Christ. [3]   John wrote of prayer to the
Son of God as a familiar ground of confidence
in Christian experience. [4]   The apostolic bene-
diction was: "The grace of our Lord Jesus
Christ, and the love of God, and the communion
of the Holy Ghost be with you all." [5]   The
whole current of adoration and devotion in the
New Testament leads up naturally and without
surprise to the magnificent words of St. Paul,
in which he speaks of "Christ, who is over all,
God blessed forever." [6]

It should be frankly recognized that the first
Christians assigned a certain subordination to
the Son in relation to the Father; but it must
be admitted with equal candour that this subordination was not in any sense a separation,

[1] Acts ix. 6.   [2] Acts ix. 13.   [3] Acts ii. 38.
[4] I John v. 13–15.   [5] 2 Cor. xiii. 14.
[6] Rom. ix. 5.   Cf. Stevens, *The Pauline Theology*, p. 201,
for a succinct statement of the grounds on which this interpretation of the text is preferred.

and that it really implied and involved a unity between them which made it possible and natural and inevitable for the disciples to pay an adoration to the Son with the Father, which, if it had been offered to, or claimed by, the greatest and best of the apostles, would have been instantly repudiated by the whole Church as not only absurd but radically blasphemous.

It is an easy matter to trace the worship of Christ in the later development of Christianity. There are two sources of evidence : the Christian hymns and liturgies ; the heathen attacks and the apologies which they evoked.

The earliest hymns of the Greek Church, the "Thanksgiving at lamplighting," "Shepherd of tender youth," "The Bridegroom cometh," the "Hymn to Christ after Silence," celebrate the praise of the Lord Jesus. Syriac poetry, through its great poet, Ephrem Syrus, takes up the same strain of adoration to the Son of God, and its undying music may still be heard among the mountains of Armenia where the unspeakable Turk is exterminating a whole race for loyalty to the name of Christ. Latin hymnody, from its earliest origin in translations from the Greek like the *Gloria in Excelsis* and the *Te Deum*, through its splendid unfolding in the poetry of Hilary of Poictiers, Ambrose of Milan, and

The testimony of the hymns.

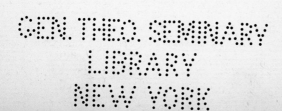

Gregory the Great, to its sweet culmination in the two Bernards, him of Clairvaux and him of Cluny, repeats the same burden :

> " O Jesus, Thou the glory art
> Of angel worlds above ;
> Thy name is music to my heart,
> Enchanting it with love."

In every land and language, in German, in French, in English, the most precious and potent melodies of the Church are fragrant with the name of Christ.

The testimony of the early liturgies.

The early liturgies bear the same testimony to the pre-eminence of the Lord Jesus in the doxologies and supplications of Christian faith. The Apostolical Constitutions,[1] the liturgy of St. James,[2] the liturgy of St. Mark,[3] the liturgy of St. Adæus and St. Maris,[4] unquestionably preserve the spirit of the early Christian worship; and they all are witnesses to the fact that the Christians prayed directly to Christ. Indeed, it lies upon the very surface of history that the growth of Christianity, as manifested

[1] *Apost. Const.*, Book VIII., chap. vii.

[2] *The Divine Liturgy of St. James*, iii.: "Sovereign Lord Jesus Christ, O Word of God," etc.

[3] *The Divine Liturgy of the Holy Apostle and Evangelist Mark*, v., xxii., etc.

[4] *Liturgy of the Blessed Apostles, composed by St. Adæus and St. Maris*, xiv.

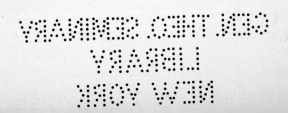

in a spreading worship, was not simply the increase of those who were willing to adore God on the authority of Christ. It was distinctly and essentially the diffusion of an inward force which impelled men to blend the name of Christ with the name of God in their prayers, and to worship the Son with the Father. The beautiful Prayer of St. Chrysostom, which closes the Litany and the Morning and Evening Prayers of the Protestant Episcopal Church, is addressed to Christ, "who dost promise that when two or three are gathered together in Thy name, Thou wilt grant their requests." [1] There is not in the world to-day a single great liturgy, Greek, Roman, Armenian, French, German, Scotch, or English, which does not contain ascriptions of divine glory, and petitions for divine grace, addressed to Jesus Christ.

Heathen writers of very early date assure us that this was the practice of Christians from the beginning. The younger Pliny reported to the Emperor Trajan that the people called Christians were accustomed to assemble before daybreak and "sing a hymn of praise responsively to Christ, as it were to God." [2] In the

The testimony of the heathen.

---

[1] St. Matt. xviii. 20.

[2] A.D. 112. See the chapter on "Pliny's Report and Trajan's Rescript" in Ramsay, *The Church in the Roman Empire* (New York, Putnam, 1893), pp. 196 ff.

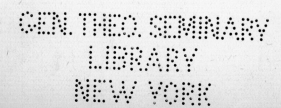

public trials that followed there was never any
denial of this statement.   It was admitted alike
by those who apostatized under the pressure of
persecution and by those who remained faithful
to the name of Christ.   The Emperor Hadrian
wrote to Servian that of the population of Alex-
andria "some worshipped Serapis, and others
Christ."   Lucian, the pagan satirist, says in
his biography of Peregrinus Proteus : " The
Christians are still worshipping that great man
who was crucified in Palestine."[1]

Christians
despised for
worshipping
Christ.

In all the apologies for the Christian religion
which were put forth during the persecutions
under Hadrian, and his successors Antoninus
Pius and Marcus Aurelius, there was no attempt to refute the universal charge that the
Christians worshipped Christ.[2]   As if to confirm this evidence by one of those indications
which are all the more significant because they
are so slight and so clearly unpremeditated,
there still exists a rude caricature, scratched
by some careless hand upon the walls of the

[1] *Luciani Samosatensis Opera.* (Ed. Leipsic, 1829), Tomus
iv., p. 173.
[2] *The First Apology of Justin Martyr*, chap. xiii. : " Our
teacher of these things is Jesus Christ ; and that we reason-
ably worship Him, having learned that He is the Son of the
true God Himself, and holding Him in the second place, and
the prophetic Spirit in the third, we will prove."

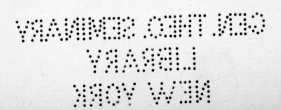

Palatine Palace in Rome not later than the beginning of the third century, representing a human figure with an ass's head hanging upon a cross, while a man stands before it in the attitude of worship.   Underneath is this ill-spelled inscription, —

" Alexamenos adore his God." [1]

Thus the songs and prayers of believers, the accusations of persecutors, the sneers of scep tics, and the coarse jests of mockers all join in proving beyond a doubt that the primitive Christians paid divine honour to the Lord Jesus. I do not see how any man can be in touch with Christianity as a living form of worship in the world, unless he knows the reality and appreciates the force of this un-questionable fact.

III

Nor will it be possible to understand the intellectual and moral teachings of the Christian religion, as they are recorded in the New Testament, unless we put ourselves at the focal point from which, as a matter of history, these teachings were first conceived and then un-

Christ was a new theology.

---

[1] *Das Spott-Crucifix der Römischen Kaiser Paläste,* Ferdinand Becker (Gera, 1876). *Das Spott-Crucifix vom Palatin,* Franz Xaver Kraus (Freiburg, 1872).

folded. This point was the vision of an unveiling of the being and mind of God in
Christ. It was not merely that Jesus said
certain things about God which men had not
known, or had forgotten. It was that they
saw in the coming of Christ a personal revelation of the Divine Being. And this revelation
touched and transformed every possible sphere
of thought and feeling in regard to the problems of religion. The personality of God was
made distinct and luminous, not only by the
recognition of an eternal Fatherhood in His
nature, but by the light of the knowledge of
His glory shining in the face of a person.[1]
The righteousness of God was disclosed in a
new aspect by the thought that He had sent
His own Son in the likeness of sinful flesh, and
for sin to condemn sin in the flesh.[2] The goodness of God was confirmed and made sufficient
for all possible human needs by the conviction
that He who spared not His own Son, but freely
delivered Him up for us all, would also with
Him freely give us all things.[3] The saving
will and power of God were apprehended
through the vision of Him in Christ reconciling the world to Himself.[4] The everlasting

[1] 2 Cor. iv. 6.
[2] Rom. viii. 3.
[3] Rom. viii. 32.
[4] 2 Cor. v. 19.

and inseparable love of God became the sure
ground of hope only when it was seen embodied in Christ Jesus our Lord.[1] The true
meaning of filial obedience to God and of
union with God was interpreted in the light
of conformity to the image of His Son.[2] And
the immense significance of immortality was
comprehended in the possession of a life hid
with Christ in God.[3]

Now the window through which men caught
sight of these truths was, and could have been,
nothing else than faith in a real incarnation
of God in Christ. The personal, moral, sympathetic view of God which distinguished the
early Church was seen only through that opening.[4] She saw the Divine Being beaming with
a new radiance, she saw the wide landscape of
human duty and destiny illuminated and transfigured, she saw a new heaven and a new earth,
when she saw in Christ all the fulness of the
Godhead dwelling bodily. And it was in the

*God was
seen through
Christ.*

---

[1] Rom. viii. 39.   [2] Rom. viii. 29.   [3] Col. iii. 3.

[4] *First Epistle of St. Clement*, chap. xxxvi. : " By Him
we look up to the heights of heaven. By Him we behold,
as in a glass, His immaculate and most excellent visage. By
Him are the eyes of our heart opened. By Him our foolish
and darkened understanding blossoms up anew towards the
light." Bp. Lightfoot's Edition. (Macmillan, 1890.)

strength and enthusiasm of this vision, that she concentrated all her moral and intellectual energies on the one point of keeping that window open, and maintaining against direct assault and secret dissolution the real and personal Deity of Christ.

IV

Christian doctrine grew around the Deity of Christ.

I am careful to put the statement in this form because I believe that it alone corresponds with the facts, and because it is only by getting our minds into this position that we can hope to understand the course, the meaning, and the force of Christian doctrine. The early Christians looked at God through Christ: they did not look at Christ through a preconceived idea and a logical definition of God. The true development of theology, to put the matter plainly, was not abstract, it was personal and practical. The doctrine of the Trinity came into being to meet an imperious necessity. That necessity was the defence of the actual worship of Christ, the actual trust in Christ as the Unveiler of the Father, which already existed at the heart of Christianity. It was recognized instinctively that the loss of this trust, the silencing of this worship,

meant the death of Christianity by heart-fail-
ure. Every speculation which threatened this
result, every theory of human nature or of
divine nature which seemed to separate the
personality of Christ from the personality of
God, was regarded by the Church as dangerous
and hostile. Every attempted statement of
theological dogma which appeared to obscure
or to imperil the reality and the eternal validity of the unveiling of the Father in the Son,
was resented, and a counter statement of theological dogma was framed to meet it. This
was the intellectual conflict of Christianity in
the first centuries: a struggle for life centring
about the actual Deity of Christ.

As we trace the progress of this conflict, *The conflict*
its vital importance emerges more and more *with heresy*
clearly. Often, I suppose, we cannot help feeling a sense of sympathy with the earnest purpose and the personal character of those men
who were called heretics. Often we are conscious of a certain distrust for the metaphysical and exegetical arguments, and of a
grave repugnance for the physical and political methods, which were used by the orthodox
to enforce their definitions. Athanasius was
not an altogether lovely person. Some of the
early Church Councils were almost as disor-

derly and reckless as some of the regiments that
have fought in various wars to defend the cause
of human liberty and justice. But the question
is not one of the manner of defence or attack.
It is a question of the reality and significance of
the cause attacked and defended.   And here we
see that Athanasius with all his faults was on
the right side, and Arius with all his virtues
was on the wrong side.   Through all the confusion of metaphysical dispute about the exact
meaning of substance and subsistence, nature
and personality, ideal existence and real existence, — terms which, as I conceive them, must
change their significance as the methods of
human philosophy change, and must always
represent imperfectly a mystery which is for
us unsearchable and indefinable, — through all
this confusion one fact shines out clear and dis-
The Palla-
dium of
Christian-
ity.
tinct.   The unveiling of the Father in Christ
was, and continued to be, and still is, the
Palladium of Christianity.   All who have surrendered it, for whatever reason, have been
dispersed and scattered.   All who have defended it, in whatever method, have been held
fast in the unity of the faith and of the knowledge of the Son of God.[1]

[1] Eph. iv. 13.

This point of view must condition the attitude of our minds towards the doctrine of the Trinity. No Christian man can be hostile or indifferent to it when he remembers its history. It may have been too much elaborated by minds over-curious in metaphysical distinctions. It may have been put in a position of undue pre-eminence by theologians whose energies were all absorbed in its construction and in the contemplation of the work of their own reason in the service of Christianity. But in spite of all excesses and errors, it stands as an enduring monument of the loyalty of the faith to its central conviction. In all its forms, from the sharply tri-personal Trinity of Athanasius, to the essentially tri-modal Trinity of Augustine, the great service which it has rendered is not abstract nor philosophical. It is practical. It has protected the conviction that the real nature of God is revealed in Christ; it has justified the consciousness that the Spirit of Christ, animating the Christian life, is the Spirit of God; it has preserved the sense of real communion with God in Christ which is the nerve of Christian worship.

And yet the doctrine of the Trinity is not the gospel, nor is it the foundation of the gospel. It cannot be preached as a saving message to the

The doctrine of the Trinity constructed to defend the Deity of Christ.

*The doc-
trine of the
Trinity
subordinate
to the gos-
pel.*

souls of men, except in that form in which we find
it in Phillips Brooks' noble *Sermon for Trinity
Sunday*, and Dr. George A. Gordon's powerful
discourse on *The Trinity the Ground of Humanity*.
It is the effort to apprehend a relation of the
Being of God to the conscious experience of
man; a truth exhibited in the course of revelation and recognized in its mysterious unfolding
both before and after all efforts to symbolize
it in theological language; in brief, it is the
reaching out of the human mind, conscious of
its limitations and conditions, towards a vision
and worship of the Father in the Son through
the Spirit. The doctrine of the Trinity is not
the Palladium. It is the defence. I will confess that in its broad outlines it seems to me
necessary and satisfactory. I will confess that
no other answer to the profound questions
which inevitably arise out of the contact between the idea of God, and the experience of
real life in all its manifoldness, appears to me
half so reasonable or complete as that which
asserts that " the various fundamental forms of
society on the earth, the essential relationships
of humanity, have their Archetype, their Eternal Pattern and Causal Source, in the nature of
the Infinite." [1]   I will confess that the form of

[1] Gordon, *The Christ of To-day*, p. 101.

this answer which contemplates the existence
of these eternal relationships in the Divine
nature as most clearly and positively personal,
is more conclusive to my mind than any other.
But if other men think otherwise on this point,
we are not therefore divided from each other,
or from the Christian faith. The question is
one of metaphysics. It is not a question of religion. All modes of defining the Trinity as a
doctrine must be kept subordinate to the purpose for which it exists. All attempts to express it are valuable only in so far as they help
us to keep in view the unveiling of the Divine
nature which centres in Him who was manifested in the flesh, justified in the Spirit, seen
of angels, preached among the nations, believed
on in the world, received up in glory.[1]

V

Now wherein is a message like this, the gospel of a personal unveiling of God in the person of Christ, adapted to the needs of the
present age?

The gospel of the Incarnation adapted to this age.

1. It seems to me first of all that the course
of modern thought has prepared the way for it
by destroying the *a priori* objections to the In-

[1] 1 Tim. iii. 16.

carnation.   Shallow agnosticism makes two assumptions which are contradictory.   It assumes
that man is unable to attain to the knowledge
of God ; and that it is impossible for God to
reveal Himself to man.   But if we cannot
know Him, how can we know that He cannot
reveal Himself?   This would be in effect the
most intimate kind of knowledge.   To take it
for granted that an Incarnation of God is impossible or incredible is to profess a most perfect and exclusive understanding of the Divine
nature.   "At one time," says Mr. Romanes,
"it seemed to me impossible that any proposition, verbally intelligible as such, could be
more violently absurd than that of the Incarnation.   Now I see that this standpoint is wholly
irrational. . . .   'But the Incarnation is opposed to common sense.'   No doubt : utterly
so ; but so it ought to be if true.   Common
sense is merely a rough register of common
experience.   But the Incarnation, if it ever
took place, whatever else it may have been,
was not a common event.   'But it is deroga-
tory to God to become man.'   How do you
know?   Besides, Christ was not an ordinary
man.   Both negative criticism and the positive
effects of His life prove this ; while if we for a
moment adopt the Christian point of view for

the sake of argument, the whole *raison d'être* of mankind is bound up in Him. Lastly, there are considerations *per contra*, rendering an Incarnation antecedently probable." [1]

2. Now these considerations to which Romanes alludes are not foreign to the intellectual atmosphere of our age; they are native to it; they are in fact the offspring of the times, born of the spirit which now leads the best thoughts of men.

The whole doctrine of development, as it is conceived by the deepest and clearest minds, looks forward to the discovery of an Incarnation which shall be at once the crown and the completion of the process of natural evolution. If nature is an orderly and progressive manifestation of an Unseen Power; if each successive step in this manifestation realizes and exhibits something higher and more perfect, to which all that has gone before has pointed, and in which the potentialities of all previous developments are not only summed up, but raised to a new power; if the mechanical structure of inorganic substances contains a prophecy (only to be interpreted after the event) of organic life, and organic life is a basis for instinct and the elementary processes of intellect,

Evolution points towards it.

[1] *Thoughts on Religion*, p. 186.

and the rude forms of thought and feeling in the lower animals foreshadow the unfolding of reflective reason and moral consciousness in man, — then surely this reflective reason and this moral consciousness, in themselves confessedly imperfect, must be only the foundation for a fuller and more perfect manifestation of that Unseen Power out of whose depths all preceding manifestations have come forth. And if the universal verdict of human science and philosophy is correct in assuming that the lower must precede the higher, and that organic life is above inorganic life, and that reason is above instinct, and that virtue is above automatic action, then it is to be expected that the complete manifestation of that Unseen Power which makes for Reason and Righteousness will neither be omitted nor intruded before its time. It cannot come too soon, without violating the order of evolution. It cannot fail to come, without destroying the significance of evolution.

Personality the final revelation.

But in what form can it come except in one which at once sums up all that has gone before it, and advances to a new level? If the universe contains an unveiling of the might, and wisdom, and reasonableness, and righteousness, of its Primal Cause, then certainly it must con-

tain at last an unveiling of His personality.
This is the only thing that remains to be
added. This is the only thing that embraces
all the rest and raises it to a new power. The
highest category known to our minds is that
of self-conscious life. Without the conception
of a personal God, man's view of the universe
must remain forever incomplete, incoherent,
and unreasonable. Without the revelation of
a personal God, the process of evolution as the
unfolding of the real secret of the universe
must remain unfinished and futile. Philosophy
as well as religion pushes us forward to this
conclusion. Personality is the ultimate reality.
Personality must be the final revelation. But
a person can be unveiled only in a personal
form. Therefore all the presumptions of reason are in favour of an Incarnation of the
Deity, not outside of nature, but in nature, to
consummate and crown that visible evolution
whereby the invisible things of Him from the
creation of the world are clearly seen. And
all the processes of intelligence are satisfied,
and rest and repose in the conviction that
the Word, which was in the beginning with
God and which was God and by whom all
things were made, finally became flesh and
dwelt among us, revealing His glory, the glory

as of the only-begotten of the Father, full of grace and truth.[1]

The gospel of the Incarnation is historically consistent.

3. Moreover, this view of Christ is adapted to the present age because it is historically consistent. We have seen that it underlies the very existence and growth of the Christian Church. The testimony of eighteen centuries to the impossibility of explaining the personality of Christ on humanitarian grounds is in itself an evidence of His divinity.

Lincoln was right when he said : " You can fool some of the people all of the time, and all of the people some of the time, but you cannot fool all of the people all of the time." A thousand attempts to account for the life of Christ without admitting His divinity have been made. Not one of them has succeeded in winning the assent and approbation of any great mass of men for any great length of time. They have hardly survived the lives of those who have invented them. Each new naturalistic theory of Christ has discredited and demolished its predecessors. And if any one of them is alive and finds credence to-day, it is only because it is the latest, and it is but

[1] See Lyman Abbott, *The Evolution of Christianity* (Houghton, Mifflin & Co., 1894), " Christ is not the product of evolution, but the producer," pp. 240–242.

waiting for its successor (as the theory of Socinus waited for the theory of Strauss, and the theory of Strauss for the theory of Renan) to be its judge and destroyer.

Meantime historic Christianity, which be- holds God incarnate in Christ, stands as a rock around which the tides of opinion ebb and flow. *The impregnable rock of Christianity.* The Church has changed in some things, but not in this. It has modified, enlarged, dimin- ished, or abandoned some articles of faith, but not this. If it be an error, it is such an error as the world has never seen anywhere else; for it has not only stood firm through the fiercest and most persistent storm of criticism that has ever been directed against any human opinion, but it has also been the foundation of the strongest and saintliest lives that humanity has ever known. If it be a truth, it must be for every Christian preacher the central truth. For it is certain that this age of ours, with its ruthless critical spirit, with its keen histori- cal sense, will never respect the intelligence, though it may acknowledge the good inten- tions, of a man who professes to speak in the name of Christianity without proclaiming, as the core of his message, the Divine Christ.

4. And this gospel meets the need of our times because it is the satisfaction of humanity.

More urgent and painful even than the questions of the intellect in regard to the being and nature of God, are the misgivings of the heart in regard to His relations to us. If He is that remote and inaccessible Sovereign

> "Who sees with equal eyes, as Lord of all,
> A hero perish or a sparrow fall,"

what possible answer can we find in Him to the longings and desires of our souls for a Divine love? what possible support can we find in Him for our struggles against outward temptation and indwelling evil? what possible sympathy can we find in Him for our hopes and aspirations and upward strivings, out of the quicksands of heredity and environment, towards liberty and light? The religion of the Incarnation is the only one that brings us near to Him, assures us of our kinship with Him, and of His infinite, practical, helpful love for us. This faith alone bridges the chasm that divides the eternal self-existent Spirit from our finite, despondent, earthbound souls. This faith alone gives us any knowledge of the things that we most need to know about Him. Deism is like a message written in an inscrutable hieroglyph which conveys no clear meaning to the mind. Theism is like a message which is intelligible to the intellect, but unsatisfactory to the heart, because it has no personal address and no signature. Christianity is a personal message, signed by the hand of a Father, and conveyed to us by the hand of the Son.

The comparison is imperfect. It falls far short of the truth. In Christianity the messenger is the message. The love which sent and the love which delivered it are the same. Christ is Immanuel, God with us. The gospel of the Incarnation does not profess to remove all intellectual perplexities in regard to the existence of God and our own souls. It professes simply to establish such a conscious relation between our souls and God that our ethical needs shall be satisfied at once; and thus it shall be infinitely easier, either to dissolve, or to endure, our intellectual perplexities. This relation is possible only in Christ. And it is possible in Him only when we receive Him as the unveiling of the Father. This requires an act of faith. But it is a faith which is simpler in its form, more natural in its method, and more profound in its spiritual results than any other. For in the last analysis it is just an act of personal confidence in a person. And this does not demand perfect knowledge, but absolute trust.

Christ is God with us.

To imagine that we can adapt our preaching to this age of doubt by weakening, concealing, or abandoning the truth of the Deity of Christ is to mistake the great need of our times. It is to seek to commend our gospel by taking away from it the chief thing that men really want, — an assurance of sympathy and kinship with God. "One of the great marks of the youth of to-day," says Ernest Lavisse, — "I speak of thinking youth, — is a longing for the Divine."[1] This longing is to be met not by slighting, but by emphasizing, not by clouding, but by clarifying, not by withdrawing, but by advancing, the true Deity of our Lord Jesus Christ. Let us take up the words of the ancient creed: "*We believe in one Lord Jesus Christ, the Son of God, only-begotten of the Father, that is of the substance of the Father, God of God, Light of Light, very God of God, begotten, not made, being of one substance with the Father: by Whom all things were made which are in heaven and earth: Who, for us men and for our salvation, came down, and was incarnate, and was made man, and suffered, and rose the third day, and ascended into the heavens, and shall come to judge the quick and the dead.*"[2]

[1] Ernest Lavisse, *La Génération de 1890.*

[2] Symbolum Nicænum, *The Creeds of Christendom*, Vol. ii. (Harpers, 1882).

IV

THE HUMAN LIFE OF GOD

"Behold Him now where He comes!
   Not the Christ of our subtle creeds,
   But the light of our hearts, of our homes,
   Of our hopes, our prayers, our needs;
   The brother of want and blame,
   The lover of women and men,
   With a love that puts to shame
   All passions of mortal ken.

*   *   *   *   *   *

"Ah no, thou life of the heart,
   Never shalt thou depart!
   Not till the leaven of God
   Shall lighten each human clod;
   Not till the world shall climb
   To thy height serene, sublime,
   Shall the Christ who enters our door
   Pass to return no more."

— RICHARD WATSON GILDER,
        The Passing of Christ.

IV

THE HUMAN LIFE OF GOD

NEARLY fifty years ago, Horace Bushnell, *A great* *truth in* the most mystical of logicians, or the most logi- *eclipse.* cal of mystics, delivered before Yale University a magnificent discourse upon *The Divinity of Christ*. In that fine work of genius, wrought out of darkness and light, mystery and clearness, like an intricate carving of ebony and gold, I find these words: "Christ is in such a sense God, or God manifested, that the unknown term of His nature, that which we are most in doubt of, and about which we are least capable of any positive affirmation, is the human." [1]

This sentence, it seems to me, is not of light, but of darkness. It does not represent that illuminating and harmonious kind of truth which comes directly from the divine revelation of Christ. It belongs rather to that obscured

[1] Horace Bushnell, *God in Christ* (New York, Scribners, 1887), p. 123.

and discordant manner of presenting truth
which is the consequence of studying it too
much at second-hand and too little at first-
hand, too much in the speculations and reason-
ings of men and too little in the facts of life
wherein it was first manifested.   Whatever
may be said of this sentence as a statement of
the result of dogmatic theology, — and in this
sense I, for one, do not question its accuracy,
—when we consider its plain meaning as an
expression of Christian experience and faith,
one thing is clear : It is utterly out of touch
with the experience and faith of the first disciples.   It is in sharp and striking discord
with the consciousness of the primitive Church.
For if there is anything in regard to which the
New Testament makes positive and undoubting
affirmation, it is the complete, genuine, and
veritable humanity of Christ.   If there is any
fact which stands out luminous and distinct
in the experience of the early Christians, it is
that they saw in Christ, not merely a mysterious manifestation of the Divine in a form calculated to beget new doubts, and under conditions which must remain inscrutable and
incomprehensible, but something utterly different.   They saw the mystery reduced to terms
of simplicity, the revelation levelled to the

*Theology
has lost
sight of
Christ's
humanity.*

direct apprehension of man, the unveiling of the Father under conditions which were so familiar that they dissolved doubts and difficulties. They saw in Christ the human life of God.

The object of this lecture is, first, to trace very briefly the way in which this view of Christ has been beclouded so that His humanity has appeared doubtful and less capable of positive affirmation; second, to show how the primitive view of His person and life may be, and in the history of Christian faith often has been, recovered and restored to its pristine brilliancy and beauty; and third, to try to express, though but imperfectly, the meaning and importance of this view for the present age.

How shall the vision be restored?

I

Definition is dangerous. Necessary it may be; useful it undoubtedly is; but our recognition of these qualities ought not to make us forget or deny the peril which the process certainly involves. And this is the nature of the danger: the definition has an inherent tendency to substitute itself for the thing defined. The terms in which a fact is expressed creep into the place of the fact itself. The reality is

Obscuration by formulas

removed insensibly to a remote distance behind the verbal symbols which represent it. The way of access to it is blocked, and its influence is restricted by the forms of expression invented to define it.

An illustration from the history of Art.

I do not know where we can find a more vivid illustration of this process than that which is given, in many ways, in the history of art. The first effort of the artist is to represent something that he has seen or imagined. Out of this effort and the work which it produces, grow certain methods and habits of representing landscape and architecture and the human figure. Out of these habits grow rules and formulas, not only for the hand but also for the eye. On these formulas schools are founded. In these schools the example of masters comes to have an authority which overshadows and limits the vision of facts as well as the representation of them. The Japanese artists, of certain schools, actually reproduce that infantile condition of sight in which all things appear flat, in a single plane, without perspective. The Giotteschi of Italy carried their disregard of anatomy to such a point that joints and articulations vanished from the human figure.

Now this same process of limitation by formulas may be observed, on the ideal side, in the course of religious art. The first pictures of Christ, traced in colour upon the walls of the Catacombs, or carved in stone upon the sarcophagi of the Christian dead, do not give us indeed the very earliest conception of Him; for the Christian art of the first two centuries, if it ever existed, has long since perished. But that which remains, dating from the third and fourth centuries, bears witness to an idea of the Christ which was simple and natural and humane. He appears as a figure of youthful beauty and graciousness; the good Shepherd bearing a lamb upon His shoulders; the true Orpheus drawing all creatures and souls by the charm of His amiable music.[1] These are only symbolic representations, yet they evidence a conception of Him which was still in touch with the facts. A little later we find an effort to conceive and depict Him with more realism. His face appears in pictures which resemble the description given in the spurious Epistle of Lentulus: "A man of dignified presence, with dark hair parted in the middle and flowing down, after the custom of the Naza-

Representations of Christ.

[1] So in the paintings from the Catacombs of *S. Agnese* and *S. Callisto.*

K

renes, over both shoulders ; His brow clear
and pure ; His unfurrowed face of pleasant
aspect and medium complexion ; His mouth
and nose faultless ; His short, light beard
parted in the middle ; His eyes bright and
lustrous."[1]

Tradition petrifies Christian Art.

But when we pass on to the creations of so-
called Byzantine art, we find ourselves face to
face with an utterly different view of the Christ.
His countenance now stares out in glittering
mosaic from the walls of great churches, huge,
dark, threatening, a dreadful and forbidding
face. The fixed and formal lines are repeated
and deepened by artist after artist. Every feature of naturalness is obliterated; every feature
that seemed to express awfulness is exagger-
ated and emphasized. The wide-set eyes, the
long narrow countenance, the stern, inflexible
mouth, — in this ocular definition the man
Christ Jesus has vanished, and we see only the
immense, immutable, and terrible Pantokrator,
who cannot be touched with the feeling of our
infirmities.[2]

When we turn to the intellectual life of the
Church out of which this type of art grew, we

[1] This is the *imago Christi* which we see in the painting
from the Catacomb of *S. Ponziano.*

[2] This type was shown in the mosaic in the Church of St.
Paul outside the walls, near Rome, lately destroyed by fire.

see there the process explained. The early
Greek Fathers, like Irenæus, went directly to
the Holy Scriptures for their view of the person of Christ, and frankly accepted all the
features of the living, lovely portrait there disclosed.   They recognized without reserve the
reality of Christ's human growth in wisdom and
stature and in favour with God and men; the
actual limitations of Christ's human knowledge
as expressed in the questions that He asked and
in His profession of ignorance in regard to the
time of His second advent; the intimacy of His
sympathy with us in temptation, suffering, and
death. But with the development of theological
definition this direct view of Christ was modified,
obscured, and at last totally eclipsed. Instead of
looking at God through His revelation in Christ,
the Fathers began to look at Christ through a
more and more abstract, precise, and inflexible
statement of the metaphysical idea of God. It
became necessary to harmonize the Scripture
record of the life of Jesus with the theories of
the divine nature set forth in the decrees of
councils and defined with amazing particularity
in the writings of theologians. In the effort to
accomplish this, two main lines of thought were
followed.   One line abandoned the belief in

*Dogmas
darken the
view of
Christ.*

Christ's real and complete humanity, and re-duced His human life to a tenuous and filmy apparition. The other line distinguished be-tween His humanity and His Divinity in such a way as to divide Him into two halves, either of which appears virtually complete without the other, and both of which are united, not in a single and sincere personality, but in an out-ward manifestation and a concealed life, cover-ing in some mysterious way a double centre of existence. It is only fair to say that the ex-treme results of these two lines of thought were condemned by the Church in the heresies of Doketism and Apollinarianism, Eutychianism and Nestorianism. But it is equally fair to say that the influence of these theories was by no means checked nor extirpated. They continued to make themselves felt powerfully and perni-ciously ; now in the direction of dissolving the humanity of Christ into a mere cloud enveloping His Deity ; and again in the direction of dividing and destroying the unity of His person in the definitions of His dual nature.

It is not necessary, nor would it be possible, for us to trace this process in detail through all its complexities and self-contradictions. It will be enough to give two or three specimens of the kind of work to which it led in dealing with two essential features of the picture of Christ which is given to us in the Gospels : His human limitation of knowledge, and His human growth in wisdom, stature, and grace. Both limitation and growth are unexempt conditions of manhood. Both are unquestionably attributed to Christ in the New Testament. Both are explicitly denied by theologians. Ephrem Syrus, commenting upon the *Diatessaron* of Tatian, says : " Christ, though He knew the moment of His advent, yet that they might not ask Him any more about it, said, *I know it not.*" [1] Chrysostom, in his explanation of St. Matthew xxiv. 36, paraphrases Christ's words in this extraordinary fashion : " For if thou seek after the day and the hour thou shalt not hear them of me, saith He ; but if of times and preludes, I will tell thee all exactly. *For that indeed I am not ignorant of it*, I have shown by many things. — I lead thee to the very vestibule ; and if I do not open unto thee the doors, this also I do for your good." [2] John of Damascus, defending the orthodox faith, declares that,

[1] *Evang. Concordant. Expos.* (Aucher and Moesinger, Venice, 1876), p. 16.

[2] St. Chrysostom, *Homilies on the Gospel of St. Matthew,* lxxvii. 2. *The Nicene Fathers* (New York, Christian Literature Co., 1888), vol. x.

" Christ is said to advance in wisdom and stature and grace, because He grows in fact in stature, and through His growth in stature brings out into exhibition the wisdom which already existed in Him. . . . But those who say that He really grew in wisdom and grace as receiving increase in these, deny that the flesh was united to the word from the first moment of its existence." [1] Peter Lombard does not explicitly adopt, but quotes with evident approval, the opinion that the person of the eternal Word put on a human body and soul as a robe, in order that He might appear suitably to the eyes of mortals, yet in Himself He was not changed by this incarnation, but remained one and the same, immutable. [2]

A very full and clear exhibition of the darkness and unreality in which the patristic and mediæval theologians involved the person of Christ may be found in Professor A. B. Bruce's great book on *The Humiliation of Christ*, [3] and in Canon Charles Gore's two admirable volumes on *The Incarnation*, [4] from which I have

---

[1] John Damascene, *De Fide Orthod.*, Lib. iii. chap. **xxii.**

[2] Peter Lombard, *Sentt.*, Book iii., Dist. vi. § 6.

[3] Prof. Alexander Balmain Bruce, *The Humiliation of Christ* (New York, Armstrongs, 1887).

[4] Canon Charles Gore, *The Incarnation of the Son of God*, Bampton Lectures, 1891 (New York, Scribners, 1891).   *Dis-*

taken some illustrations after verifying them.
Professor Bruce sums up the matter by saying:
"The effect, though not the design, of theories
of Christ's person has been to a large extent to
obscure some of these elementary truths, —
the unity of the person, or the reality of the
humanity, or the divinity dwelling within the
man, or the voluntariness and ethical value of
the state of the humiliation. That is, certain-
ties have been sacrificed for uncertainties, facts
for hypotheses, faith for speculation."[1]

Canon Gore, in his Bampton Lectures, *The man-
adroitly uses the Jesuit theologian De Lugo as* *hood of*
Jesus van-
a man of straw through whom he may safely *ishes.*
and vigorously attack the false conceptions of
Christ's person which are still current, and to a
considerable degree dominant, in dogmatic theology. He says that De Lugo depicts a Christ
"who, if He was, as far as His body is con-
cerned, in a condition of growth, was, as re-
gards His soul and intellect, from the first
moment and throughout His life in full enjoy-
ment of the beatific vision. Externally a way-
farer, a *viator*, inwardly He was throughout
a *comprehensor*, He had already attained. . . .
It is denied that He can be strictly called

sertations on *Subjects connected with the Incarnation* (New
York, Scribners, 1895). [1] *The Humiliation of Christ*, p. 192.

' the servant of God ' even as man, in spite of the direct use of that expression in the Acts of the Apostles. He is spoken of at the institution of the Eucharist as offering sacrifice to His own Godhead." [1]

Modern ex-
amples of
false Chris-
tology.

Canon Gore condemns this picture by De Lugo as in striking contradiction to that which the New Testament presents. But the point which I wish to make clear and distinct, is that, in spite of this contradiction, the picture has not been frankly and finally discarded in Christian theology. It still exercises an obscuring and perverting influence upon the vision of Christ. It still produces, by imitation, representations of Him in which definitions dominate facts, and formulas hide or obliterate realities. We do not need to go back to the seventeenth century, nor abroad to the Jesuits, for our examples. We may turn to Archdeacon Wilberforce's book on *The Incarnation*, and find him representing the body of Christ as miraculous in its freedom from sickness, its power over animals, its exemption from the necessity of death, and its inherent power of communicating life to others.[2] In regard to the mind of

[1] *The Incarnation*, p. 164.
[2] Archdeacon Wilberforce, *The Doctrine of the Incarnation* (New York, Young, 1885), pp. 60–65.

Christ, he says that "since it would be impious to suppose that our Lord had pretended an ignorance which He did not experience, we are led to the conclusion [astonishing conclusion!] that what He partook, as man, was not actual ignorance, but such deficiency in the means of arriving at truth as belongs to mankind."[1] We may turn to the *Dogmatic Theology* of Dr. W. G. T. Shedd and read: "Jesus Christ as a theanthropic person was constituted of a divine nature and a human nature. The divine nature had its own form of experience, like the mind in an ordinary human person; and the human nature had its own form of experience, like the body in a common man. The experiences of the divine nature were as diverse from those of the human nature as those of the human mind are from those of the human body. Yet there was but one person who was the subject-ego of both of these experiences. At the very time when Christ was conscious of weariness and thirst by the well of Samaria, He also was conscious that He was the eternal and only-begotten Son of God, the second person in the Trinity. This is proved by His words to the Samaritan woman: ' Whosoever drinketh of the water that I shall give

A double conscious- ness.

[1] *Ibid.*, p. 71.

him shall never thirst ; but the water that I shall give him shall be in him a well of water springing up into everlasting life. I that speak unto thee am the Messiah.' The first-mentioned consciousness of fatigue and thirst came through the human nature in His person ; the second-mentioned consciousness of omnipotence and supremacy came through the divine nature in His person. If He had not had a human nature, He could not have had the former consciousness; and if He had not had a divine nature, He could not have had the latter. Because He had both natures in one person, He could have both."[1] We may turn to Canon Liddon's magnificent work on *The Divinity of our Lord* and find him writing : " Christ's Manhood is not of Itself an individual being ; It is not a seat and centre of personality ; It has no conceivable existence apart from the act whereby the Eternal Word in becoming Incarnate called It into being and made It His Own. It is a vesture which He has folded around His person ; It is an instrument through which He places Himself in contact with men and whereby He acts upon humanity."[2]

His manhood a vesture.

[1] W. G. T. Shedd, *Dogmatic Theology* (New York, Scribners, 1888), vol. ii., pp. 307, 308.

[2] H. P. Liddon, *The Divinity of our Lord and Saviour Jesus Christ*, Bampton Lectures, 1866 (London, Rivingtons, 11th edition, 1885), p. 262.

And so, if we accept this picture of Christ, the manhood of Jesus fades, retreats, grows dim and shadowy. It wavers like a veil. It dissolves like mist. It descends again mysterious and impenetrable, illusory and impersonal, to envelop Him whom we love and adore in its strange and unfamiliar folds. We grope after Him, but we can touch nothing but the hem of His mystic robe. We long for Him, but He approaches us, and comes into contact with us, only through an instrument. He is not what He seems. The Son of God behind that veil is beyond our reach. The Son of man, whom human eyes beheld and human hands touched, is not the real, living, veritable Saviour, but only the form, the garment, of an inscrutable life. And if, in our dire confusion, our reasoning faith still succeeds in holding fast to the Eternal Logos, our confiding faith is maimed and robbed by the loss of that true, near, personal, loving, sympathizing Jesus, who was born of a woman, suffered under Pontius Pilate, was crucified, dead, and buried. He is gone from us, as certainly as if the Pharisees had spoken truth when they said that His disciples came by night and stole Him away. The thing of which we are most in doubt, and about which we are least capable of any positive

The human Christ is lost.

affirmation, as Dr. Bushnell said, is the humanity of Christ. We are left with a perfectly orthodox doctrine of two natures, but we no longer have a clear and simple gospel of One Person to preach to doubting men.

II

The cry of the heart for a human Saviour.

But the heart of Christendom has never rested content with this distant, vague, uncertain view of the real manhood of our Lord. There has always been a protest against it. There has always been an effort to escape from it.

The worship of the Virgin Mary.

We can see a strange and indirect but indubitable evidence of this deep inward dissatisfaction, in the rise and growth of an impassioned devotion to the human mother of Jesus. The worship of the Virgin Mary was a reprisal for the obscuration of the humanity of her Son. In the thought of her true womanly tenderness and affection, her real and unquestionable sorrows, her simple and familiar joys, her intimate, genuine, unfailing sympathy with all that makes our mortal life a bitter, blessed reality to us, the souls of the lowly and the lonely found that peace and consolation

which they could no longer find in the contemplation of the distant Second Person of the
Trinity through the telescope of theology.
That which Jesus Himself was to John and
Peter, to the household of Bethany, to the
penitent publican, and to the woman which
was a sinner, Mary became to the baffled and
confused faith of a later age, — an approachable
mediator of the divine mercy, a helper who
could really understand and feel the need of
those who cried for help, a warm and living
image of the Eternal Sympathy in flesh and
blood. In the light of mediæval dogmatics
Mariolatry appears not without its justifica-
tion. And for my part, I should not wish to be
bound to the Christology of Peter Lombard
and Thomas Aquinas, without finding the com-
pensation which their followers found in personal devotion and confidential trust, flowing
instinctively and irresistibly towards the blessed
Virgin.

But, after all, this was only a substitute for
the real thing. It gave to faith the image of
a lovely and adorable humanity in closest union
with God ; but it did not give back the old
vision of the human life of God. And so
through all the ages we see men turning, now
in solitary thought, now in great companies, to

*The search
after Jesus*

seek that vision.   The renaissance of Christian art, with its beautiful pictures of the infancy of Jesus, with its piercing and pathetic representations of the sufferings of Jesus, bears witness to the eagerness of that search.   The revivals of Christian life, seen in such diverse yet cognate forms as the rise of the " Poor Men of Lyons" and the foundation of the "Brotherhood of St. Francis" are evidences of the same movement back to Christ.   Peter Waldo outside of the Church, and Francis of Assisi within the Church, were awakened by the same vision of Jesus, "a man of sorrows and acquainted with grief," and were inspired by the same desire to make His real human life the pattern of all piety and the example of all goodness.   The Reformation, which was at once and equally an intellectual and a spiritual protest against the arrogance of current theology and the coldness of religious life, supplies no better watchword to express its great motive than the saying of Erasmus : " I could wish that those frigid subtleties either were completely cut off, or were not the only things that the theologians held as certain, and that *the Christ pure and simple might be implanted deep within the minds of men.*" [1]

The spirit of the Reformation.

[1] Erasmus, quoted in Gore, *Dissertations*, etc., p. 180, Epistle 207.

Modern Biblical scholarship, with its splendid apparatus of linguistic and historical learning, proceeding in part, at first, from a sceptical impulse, has developed in our generation, either through the conversion of sceptics in the process of research, or through the awakening of believers to the necessities of their faith, into a reverent and eager quest for the historic Christ, the Jesus of the Gospels, the Lord of the primitive Church, that we may see Him as the first Christians saw Him, in the integrity of His person and the sincerity of His life, and receive from Him what they received, — a faith that dissolved doubts and an inspiration that conquered difficulties. Back to the New Testament of our Lord and Saviour Jesus Christ, — back to the facts that lie behind the definitions, back to the Person who embodies the truth, back to the record and reflection of that which the apostles "heard, and saw with their eyes, and looked upon, and their hands handled of the word of life," — this, and this only, is the way that leads us within sight of

"Back to Christ!"

> " the heaven-drawn picture
> Of Christ, the living Word."

Now it is a marvellous thing, and one for which we can never be grateful enough, that

when we come to the New Testament in this
spirit, we find in it exactly what we need ; not an
abstract formula, not a collection of definitions,
but the graphic reflection of a Person seen
from a fourfold point of view, and the simple
record of manifold human experience under the
direct and dominant influence of that Person.
And the one fact that emerges clear and triumphant from the reflection and the record, is
that the writers of the New Testament never
were in doubt of the human nature of Christ
and never hesitated to make the most positive
affirmations in regard to it.

The Christ of the Gospels is bone of our
bone, flesh of our flesh, mind of our mind,
heart of our heart. He is in subjection to
His parents as a child. He grows to manhood. His character is unfolded and perfected
by discipline. He labours for daily bread, and
prays for Divine grace. He hungers, and
thirsts, and sleeps, and rejoices, and weeps.
He is anointed with the Spirit for His ministry. He is tempted. He is lonely and dis-
appointed. He asks for information. He
confesses ignorance. He interprets the facts
of nature and life with a prophetic insight.
But He makes no new disclosure of the secrets
of omniscience. There is no hint nor indica-

tion that He is leading a double life, reigning consciously as God while He is suffering apparently as man. His personality is simple and indivisible. The glory of what He is and does, lies not only in its perfection, but in the hard conditions of its accomplishment. Superhuman in His origin, as the only-begotten Son of God; superhuman in His office and work, as the revealer of the Father and the redeemer of mankind; in His earthly existence the Christ of the Gospels enters without reserve and without deception into all the conditions and limitations which are necessary to give to the world, once and forever, the human life of God.

When we turn to the Epistles to see how *The Christ* this view of Christ was affected by the recog- *of the* nition of His divine glory and power as one *Epistles.* who had been raised to the right hand of God and made head over all things to the Church, two things strike us with tremendous force. First, the identity of His person was not lost, nor the continuity of His being broken: the exalted Christ is none other than "this same Jesus." [1] Second, the reality and absoluteness of His humiliation are emphasized as the ground and cause of His exaltation.

How vividly these two things come out, for

[1] Acts i. 11.

L

example, in the writings of St. Paul. It has been well said that "the Christ whom Paul had seen was the risen Christ, and the conception of Him in His glorified character is the one which rules his thoughts and forms the starting-point of his teaching." [1] Corresponding to this present glory, Paul assumes an eternally pre-existent glory of Christ as the image of the invisible God, the medium and end of creation. [2] Now it is of this Person, divinely glorious in the past as the One who is before all things and in whom all things consist, [3] divinely glorious in the present as the One who is far above every name that is named, not only in this world but in that which is to come, [4] — it is of this Person that Paul writes, in words so strong that they touch the very border of the impossible: "For our sakes, *He beggared Himself* that we through His beggary might be enriched." [5] And again: "He, existing in the form of God, did not consider an equal state with God a thing to be selfishly grasped and held, but *emptied Himself*, and took the form of a slave, being made in the likeness of man." [6] These powerful expressions, "self-

[1] Stevens, *The Pauline Theology*, p. 206.
[2] Col. i. 16.   [3] Col. i. 17.   [4] Eph. i. 21.
[5] 2 Cor. viii. 9.   [6] Phil. ii. 6, 7.

beggary," "self-emptying," seem to be directly designed to break up the conventional moulds in which dogmatic theology has attempted to cast the truth and let it harden. They bring back a vital warmth and motion into the facts of the Incarnation. Once more it glows and flows. Once more we see that it is not a mere exhibition of being but a process of becoming. The idea of self-beggary mightily overflows the mere statement that a human nature was added and united to the divine nature; for that would have been no impoverishment but an enrichment. The idea of self-emptying shatters the narrow dogma that the Son of God suffered no change in Himself when He became man. It was a change so absolute, so immense, that it can only be compared with the vicissitude from fulness to emptiness. He laid aside the existence-form of God, in order that He might take the existence-form of man. Whatever right He had to an equal state of glory with God, that right He did not cling to, but surrendered, in order that He might become a servant. And upon this real self-emptying there followed a real self-humiliation, wherein, being found in fashion as a man, He became obedient unto death, even the death

The Kenosis

of the cross.[1]   It was on account of this, —
and by "this" we must understand the entire
actual operation of the self-denying, self-hum-
bling, self-sacrificing mind of Christ, — it was
for this reason, St. Paul declares, that "God
highly exalted Him, and gave unto Him the
name which is above every name."[2]   And I
know not how to interpret such language
with any reality of intelligence, unless it
means that the present glory of the Son of
God is in some true sense the result of His
having become man and so fulfilled the will
of God.

The Epistle of Christ's brotherhood.
This view, which St. Paul condenses into a
single pregnant "wherefore," is expanded in
the Epistle to the Hebrews.   The object of
this Epistle is to show the superiority of the
priesthood and sacrifice of Christ, which are
substantial and enduring, to the priesthood and
sacrifice of the old dispensation, which were
shadowy and transient.   But the method which
the writer follows is not to deny, but to assert
the verity of Christ's humanity.   Without this
He could not be the true priest nor offer the
true sacrifice.   "In all things it behoved Him
to be made like unto His brethren."[3]   "For we
have not an high priest which cannot be touched

[1] Phil. ii. 8.   [2] Phil. ii. 9.   [3] Heb. ii. 17.

with the feeling of our infirmities : but was in all points tempted like as we are, yet without sin." [1] "Though He were a Son, yet learned He obedience by the things which He suffered, and being made perfect, He became the author of eternal salvation unto all them that obey Him." [2] This complete incarnation, this thorough trial under human conditions, this perfect discipline of obedience through suffering, was a humiliation. But it was in no sense a degradation. On the contrary, it was a crowning of Christ with glory and honour in order that He might taste death for every man. "For it became Him, for whom are all things, and by whom are all things, in bringing many sons to glory, to make the captain of their salvation perfect through suffering." [3] If the Epistle to the Hebrews teaches anything, it certainly teaches this. The humanity of Jesus was not the veiling but the unveiling of the divine glory. The limitations, temptations, and sufferings of manhood were the conditions under which alone Christ could accomplish the greatest work of the Deity, — the redemption of a sinful race. The seat of the divine revelation and the centre of the divine atonement was and is the human life of God.

The glory of condescension.

[1] Heb. iv. 15.   [2] Heb. v. 8, 9.   [3] Heb. ii. 9, 10.

III

Here, then, we may pause for a moment and try to sum up the conclusions to which the New Testament leads us in regard to the person of Christ.

I am sincerely anxious not to be misunderstood. On the one hand, I would not conceal for a moment my conviction that current theology has failed, very often and very largely, to do justice to the meaning of the Incarnation on the human side, and that we *must* go back to the image of Jesus Christ as it is reflected in the Gospels to purify, and refresh, and simplify our faith. We should not suffer any reverence for ancient definitions of doctrine, however well founded, nor any fear of incurring reproach and mistrust as innovators, to deter us from that necessary and loyal return to the reality of the Person in whom our creed centres and on whom it rests. To find Jesus anew, to see Him again, as if for the first time, in the wondrous glory of His humility, is the secret of the revival of Christianity in every age. This is not innovation; it is renovation.

On the other hand, we have no right and we ought to have no inclination to insist exclusively upon any particular theory as the only possible explanation of the facts of the Incarnation. Every earnest and thoughtful man must feel that these facts are so deep and mysterious that the plummet of human reason cannot sound their ultimate recesses. With all our thinking upon this subject, there must ever mingle a consciousness of insufficiency and a confession of ignorance. But with this confession of ignorance there must go also a clear recognition of those portions of the truth which are unquestionably revealed in the New Testament. Three things are there made plain to faith.

1. God is so closely related to man, and the *Three vital* likeness of God in man is so real, that the Divine Logos is able to descend by a free act of self-determining love into the lower estate of human existence, and humble Himself to the conditions of manhood without losing His personal identity.

points.

2. The essence of the Gospel is its declaration of the fact that this act of condescension, of self-humiliation, actually has been performed, and that Jesus Christ is the eternal Son of God who has taken upon Him the existence-form of a servant, and lived a truly human life, and been obedient even unto death, in order to reveal to the world the saving love of God.

3. The distinctive attributes of personality in Christ (self-consciousness and self-determination) are not dual, as of two persons, the one divine and the other human, co-existing side by side in a double life, but individual, and manifested as the life of one person. That person is the Son of God, who laid aside the glory which He had with the Father, and emptied Himself, and so became the Son of man; and on account of this humiliation God hath highly exalted Him and crowned Him with glory and honour as the God-man forever.

These points must be defended. These are the points which are vital to the reality of the Gospel of the Incarnation. All theories which make these points clear, safeguard the truth in its integrity and in its reconciling power. The question of the method of the divine humiliation and the human exaltation of Christ, lies beyond these points. It is not necessary to insist upon any particular form of its solution. Indeed, it may well be that the profundity of the question, the inherent mystery of the facts of life and personality with which it deals, and the limitations of human thought and language, preclude the possibility of a complete and final answer at present. It must be frankly acknowledged that none of the solutions which have been propounded hitherto are free from serious perplexities. But it must be recognized with equal frankness that the theories which have been put forward in modern times, with new earnestness and power, by men of unquestionable loyalty to the Christianity of the New Testament, who have sought to find a clear and positive meaning for the great word *Kenosis*, which St. Paul uses to describe the self-emptying of Christ in the Incarnation, — theories which have been stigmatized as *kenotic*, as if the name were enough to mark them as unorthodox, — are so far from being heretical that they have the rare merit of conserving and emphasizing a truth of surpassing value, undoubtedly taught in the Bible, and too much neglected, if not practically denied, during many centuries of theological speculation. It may be, as Julius Müller held, that the distinctive attributes of personality are, abstractly considered, identical in God and man, so that, by the divine self-limitation in the Incarnation, they are actually unified, like two circles which have a common centre.[1] It may be, as Dr. Fairbairn holds, that the Son of God, being the eternal repre-

Various methods of safe-guarding them.

---

[1] For this statement of Müller's view, which he gave in his lectures, I am indebted to Dr. George P. Fisher, who was one of his hearers.

sentative of the filial relationship within the Godhead, the symbol of the created within the uncreated, needed but to surrender the form and status of the uncreated Son in order to assume, by the same act, the form and status which man as the created Son was intended to realize.[1] It may be, as Godet holds, that the Incarnation was by deprivation, and that the Eternal Word renounced His divine mode of being, and entered into life, without omniscience, omnipresence, or omnipotence, as an unconscious babe.[2] It matters little in what form of words we try to express the transcendent truth. But it matters much, it is supremely important for the integrity of our Gospel and for its influence upon the heart of this doubting age, that we should hold fast to the fact that the life of Jesus of Nazareth is simply and sincerely the human life of God.

The new study of Christ.

The time is at hand when this simple and profound view of Christ, which beholds in Him the God-man in whom Deity is self-limited and humbled in order that humanity may be divinely exalted and perfected, must break through the clouds which have obscured it, and become the leading light of religion and theol-

[1] *The Place of Christ in Modern Theology*, p. 476.
[2] Godet, *Commentary on John* i. 14.

ogy. The life of Christ needs to be restudied and rewritten under this luminous guidance, in absolute and unhesitating loyalty to the facts as they lie before our eyes in the Gospels.[1] The doctrine of Christ's person needs to be reconstructed and restated in this light. It must include, as the creed of Chalcedon included, not only the truth of a Homoöusia — a sameness of nature and experience — with God, which the past has vindicated ; but also the equal truth of a Homoöusia with man, which the future is to unfold as the universality of Christ's manhood is exhibited through His progressive triumphs among all the races of men and all the modes of human life. The humanity of the incarnate Christ must stand out as clear, as pos-

---

[1] "No *action* of our Saviour's earthly life, from Bethlehem to Calvary, exhibits divinity. He appears first as a helpless babe in the manger. He is subject to His parents. As the child grows, He waxes strong in spirit and increases in wisdom. Such an increase in wisdom implies increase in knowledge, and less knowledge or greater ignorance to-day than to-morrow. Omniscience could not have been exercised by the Jesus who was growing in wisdom. If any say here, as we usually do, that the humanity grew but the divinity was omniscient, let us ask if there were two persons in Jesus. This Nestorianism is practically the creed of the present day with the Reformed Churches. They have gone over to a virtual duplication of the person of Christ." — HOWARD CROSBY, *The True Humanity of Christ* (New York, Randolph, 1880).

itive, as indubitable, as His Deity. Nay, more, it must stand where the New Testament puts it, in the foreground of faith. For it is only in this humanity that we can truly find the Son of God who loved us and gave Himself for us.

The old definitions inadequate.

How urgent and pressing are the needs of our own age which call us to this work! How far behind us, how effete and inadequate, are the terms and illustrations which were used in former ages to express the results of human thought in regard to the person of Christ! Recall, for instance, that fine similitude of the heated sword which the Lutheran theologians borrowed from the Fathers to explain the union of the divine with the human in Christ! To them it was satisfactory because they regarded heat as one substance and iron as another substance. In their view the divine nature penetrated and pervaded the human nature as the caloric fluid was supposed to permeate a mass of metal. But in our world the caloric fluid does not exist. Heat is not a substance, but a mode of motion in substances. In the light of modern science the old similitude fades into a meaningless comparison of things which cannot be compared.

We cannot accept the scholastic terminology of "natures" and "subsistences" in the final

and absolute sense in which it was once employed. The philosophy of realism, which
ascribed an objective existence to universals
apart from individuals, is not the philosophy of
to-day. Its language is not only foreign, but
dead. The philosophy of being and not-being
has opened to receive the philosophy of becoming; and, in so doing, it has been utterly transformed.

Life is now the regnant idea; personality its *Life is the*
utmost expression. It is in the facts of life, *regnant*
its secret potencies, its mysterious limitations *idea.*
in germ and seed, its magnificent unfoldings in
the process of development that we must seek
our comparisons for the Incarnation. And the
very search will bring us face to face with the
conviction that life in all its manifestations
transcends analysis without ceasing to be the
object of knowledge.

In the living world the boundaries of imagi- *We know*
nation are not coterminous with the limits of *life but can-*
apprehension. We know many facts and *not define it.*
forms of life whose modes of becoming we
cannot imagine. It is just as impossible for
us to conceive how the life of the oak, root and
trunk and branch and leaf, form and colour
and massive strength, is all folded in the tiny,
colourless, unshaped seed, as it is to conceive

how the life of God is embodied in the man Christ Jesus. But the difficulty of conceiving the manner of this infolding, this embodiment, does not destroy for us the reality of the life. Indeed, if we could explain it entirely, if we could trace it perfectly as in a diagram, if we could observe it completely, as in one of those beautiful models of flowers which a skilful artist[1] has recently made to illustrate his lectures on botany, we should know that it was not life, but only a picture of it. The picture is useful, but it is not vital. The metaphor has its value, but it falls far short of the truth. *Self-beggary* and *self-emptying* are but "words thrown out towards" an unimaginable but not unreasonable manifestation of the Divine Love as life. The reality to which they point us is the Son of God descending to live under all the conditions and limitations of energy and consciousness which are proper to the Son of man : the Word made flesh and dwelling among us, like unto His brethren in all things.

IV

The importance of this view for the present age.

It would be hard to overestimate the significance of this view for the present age, and the importance of setting it forth as a living truth

[1] William Hamilton Gibson.

in the language of to-day.   It is the only view
which gives us any ground of reality for our
faith in the kinship of man with God.   If the
Son of God, who is the image of the Father, by
laying aside the outward prerogatives of His
divine mode of existence, actually becomes
human, then, and only then, the divine image
in which man was created is no mere figure of
speech, but a substantial likeness of spiritual
being.   There is a true fellowship between
our souls and our Father in heaven.   Virtue
is not a vain dream, but a definite striving
towards His perfection.   Revelation is not a
deception, but a message from Him who knows
all to those who know only a part.   Prayer is
not an empty form, but a real communion.

" Speak to Him, thou, for He hears, and Spirit with Spirit
    can meet:
  Closer is He than breathing, and nearer than hands
    and feet."[1]

This view of the spiritual relation of man to
God cannot possibly have any foundation in
fact, deep enough and strong enough to withstand the sweeping floods of scepticism, unless
it builds upon the rock of a veritable Incarnation.   The discoveries of modern science, en-
larging enormously our conceptions of the

*The kinship
of man to
God.*

[1] Tennyson, *The Higher Pantheism.*

physical universe, have not only put man (as we said in the first lecture) in a position to receive a larger and loftier vision of the glory of God, but they have made such a vision indispensable. And they have emphasized, with overwhelming force, the form in which that vision must come in order to meet our needs and strengthen faith for its immense task. If we are not to be utterly belittled and crushed by the contemplation of the vast mass of matter and the tremendous play of force by which we are surrounded ; if we are still to hold that the vital is greater than the mechanical, the moral than the material, the spiritual than the physical ; if we are to maintain the old position of all noble and self-revering thought, that " man is greater than the universe," — there is nothing that can so profoundly confirm and establish us, there is nothing that can so surely protect and save us from " the distorting influences of our own discoveries," as the revelation of the Supreme Being in an unmistakably vital, moral, spiritual, and human form.

The true view of God. Such a revelation at once rectifies, purifies, and elevates our view of God Himself. For if the Son of God can surrender omnipresence, omniscience, and omnipotence without destroying His personal identity, then the central essence of the Deity is neither infinite wisdom nor infinite power, but perfect holiness and perfect goodness. And so from the very lowest valley of humiliation we catch clear sight of the very loftiest summit of theology, the serene and shining truth that God is Love.

In the light of this truth we behold also the highest perfection of man and the path which leads to it. Love is the fulfilling of the law, and the supreme pattern of love is the example of Christ. And whether we look at it from the divine side as the supreme self-sacrifice of God, or from the human side as the complete obedience of man, everything depends upon the genuineness and sincerity of this example. Unless the Son of God truly became man, the Incarnation cannot be, as Bishop Westcott calls it, "a revelation of human duties." What strength could we draw from His victory over temptation if He was not exposed as we are to the assaults of evil? What consolation could we draw from His patience if He was not a man of sorrows and acquainted with grief? "Jesus Christ," says one of the greatest of French theologians, "is not the Son of God hidden in the Son of man retaining all the attributes of Divinity in a latent state. This

The supreme pattern of love.

M

would be to admit an irreducible duality which would make the unity of His person vanish and withdraw Him from the normal conditions of human life. His obedience would become illusory, and His example would be without application to our race. No, when the Word became flesh, He humbled Himself, He put off His glory, being rich He made Himself poor, and became as one of us, only without sin, that He might pass through the moral conflict with all the risks of freedom."[1] When we see Him thus, we know what it means to follow Him and to be like Him.

The value of the atonement. Finally, the whole value of the Atonement, in its reconciling influence on the heart of man, in its exhibition of the heart of God, depends upon the actuality of the Incarnation. If He who died on Calvary was a mere theophany, like the angel of Jehovah who appeared to Abraham, then His death was merely a dramatic spectacle. The body of Jesus was broken, *God suffers with and for us.* but God was not touched. But if the Father truly spared not His own Son, but delivered Him up for us all, then the Father also suffered by sympathy, making an invisible sacrifice, an infinite surrender of love for our sakes.

[1] De Pressensé, *Jésus-Christ* (Paris, 1865), Book I., chap. v., p. 254.

Then the Son also suffered, making a visible sacrifice, and pouring out His soul unto death to redeem us from the fear of death and the power of sin. And this becomes real to our faith and potent upon our souls only when we see the human life of God, agonizing in the garden, tortured in the judgment-hall, and expiring upon the cross. Then we can say

> " Oh Love Divine! that stooped to share
> Our sharpest pang, our bitterest tear."

Then we can look up to a God who is not impassible, as the speculations of men have falsely represented Him, but passible, and therefore full of infinite capacities of pure sorrow and saving sympathy. Then the dumb and sullen resentment which rises in noble minds at the thought of a Universe in which there is so much helpless pain and hopeless grief, created by an immovable Being who has never felt and can never feel either pain or grief, — that sense of moral repulsion from the idea of an unsuffering and unsympathetic Creator which is, and always has been, the deepest, darkest spring of doubt, fades away, and we behold a God who became human in order that He might bear, though innocent and undeserving, all our pains and all our griefs.

Doubts dissolve in the thought of God's sympathy.

Thus the men who believe in the human life of God can stand before the doubting age, as David stood before the disillusioned, downcast, despondent Hebrew king, in Robert Browning's splendid poem of "Saul." The word, sought in vain among the glories of nature, among the joys of human intercourse, the word of faith and hope and love and life, comes to us, leaps upon us, flashes through us.

"See the King — I would help him, but cannot, the
     wishes fall through.
Could I wrestle to raise him from sorrow, grow poor
     to enrich,
To fill up his life, starve my own out, I would — know-
     ing which,
I know that my service is perfect. Oh, speak through
     me now !
Would I suffer for him that I love? So wouldst
     Thou — so wilt Thou !
So shall crown Thee the topmost, ineffablest, uttermost
     crown —
And Thy love fill infinitude wholly, nor leave up nor
     down
One spot for the creature to stand in ! It is by no
     breath,
Turn of eye, wave of hand, that salvation joins issue
     with death !
As Thy Love is discovered almighty, almighty be
     proved
Thy power, that exists with and for it, of being be-
     loved !
He who did most, shall bear most; the strongest shall
     stand the most weak.

'Tis the weakness in strength, that I cry for! my flesh,
     that I seek
In the Godhead! I seek and I find it. O Saul, it
     shall be
A Face like my face that receives thee; a Man like
     to me,
Thou shalt love and be loved by, forever; a Hand
     like this hand
Shall throw open the gates of new life to thee!
     See the Christ stand!"

THE SOURCE OF AUTHORITY IN
THE KINGDOM OF HEAVEN

" But Thee, but Thee, O sovereign Seer of time,
  But Thee, O poets' Poet, Wisdom's Tongue,
  But Thee, O man's best Man, O love's best Love,
  O perfect life in perfect labour writ,
  O all men's Comrade, Servant, King, or Priest, —
  What *if* or *yet*, what mole, what flaw, what lapse,
  What least defect or shadow of defect,
  What rumour, tattled by an enemy,
  Of inference loose, what lack of grace
  Even in torture's grasp, or sleep's, or death's, —
  Oh, what amiss may I forgive in Thee,
  Jesus, good Paragon, thou Crystal Christ?"

                — SIDNEY LANIER, *The Crystal.*

V

THE SOURCE OF AUTHORITY IN THE KINGDOM OF HEAVEN

PREACH CHRIST, is the apostolic watchword *The new command-* that rings to-day, with all the force and charm *ment.* of a new commandment, through the heart of a Church, which has felt, more deeply than it has yet confessed, the age-pervading chill of a winter of doubt and discontent. The very entrance of that mystic and reviving word has already brought a glow of enthusiasm into the Christian life, and caused new blossoms of hope and love, manifold and beautiful activities of help and healing, to appear in the earth. It seems as if some fresh and secret tide of vitality were flowing through the veins of Christendom, and breaking everywhere towards the light in deeds of charity and enterprises of mercy. Hospitals, asylums, red cross societies, rescue missions, salvation armies, spring into existence as if by magic. Never has there been a time when Christian men have tried to

*The new
charity.*

do so much for their fellow-men in the name
and for the sake of Christ. Never has there
been a time when they have recognized so
clearly and fully that there was so much yet
to be done. It is an age of secular doubt, as
many other ages have been. But it is also an
age of Christian beneficence, as hardly any
other age has been. And this beneficence is
not self-satisfied and complacent. It is self-
reproachful, and, in its best expressions, nobly
discontented with all that has been accomplished hitherto. It seeks, not always wisely,
but with splendid eagerness, for plans which
shall lead beyond the relief, to the prevention
of human suffering. It aims to bring about
not only the immediate mitigation, but also the
ultimate abolition, of war. It demands that
charity shall be translated into the terms of
national, as well as of individual life. It will
not be satisfied until in some real and palpable
sense the kingdom of this world is become the
kingdom of our Lord and of His Christ.[1]

*Christ is the
fountain.*

Now this renewal, this splendid expansion of
Christian activities, evident by many signs to
all thoughtful observers, depends for its power
and permanence upon the setting forth of
Christ, vividly, personally, practically, as the

[1] Rev. xi. 15.

pattern of all virtue and the Prince of Peace
among men.   The sense of absolute confidence
in Him as the perfect example of goodness, and
of thorough loyalty to Him as the Master of
noble life, is the hidden reservoir of moral
force.   The organized charities of Christendom
are the distributing system.   Not more instant
and more complete would be the water-famine
on Manhattan Island if the great dam among
the Croton hills were broken and all the lakes
and streams dried up, than the drought that
would fall upon the beneficence of the world if
there were a sudden break in the reservoir of
love and loyalty in Christian hearts to their
moral Master, or a stoppage of the myriad and
multiform feeders which keep it full by preaching Christ.

But in all this renewal and expansion of what
is well and proudly called practical Christianity,
there is, if I mistake not, a danger, or at least
a serious possibility, of loss.   The life of man
is not only practical, it is also intellectual.   His
relations to his fellow-men are important, but
his relation to truth is no less important.   He
cannot help acting ; neither can he help thinking.   When his thinking is divorced from his
acting, when he has one standard for truth and
a different standard for conduct, he is like a

*The peril of
practical
Christianity*

house divided against itself. If the Christianity of to-day, by dwelling exclusively or too much on the ethical side of the Gospel as a beautiful and beneficent rule of conduct illustrated by a perfect Example, tends to ignore the intellectual necessities of man and fails to realize that it has a message to deliver in the realm of truth as well as in the realm of righteousness, it will not and it cannot meet the deepest wants of the present age. Indeed, it may even aggravate those wants and make them more painful. It may seem to give assent, by silence, to the desperate assumption of scepticism that the unseen world is unknown and unknowable, even to the most perfect of men. It may foster the sad feeling that the reality of religion is beyond our reach and that we must content ourselves with the convenient dreams of virtue. It may preach, in effect, a Christ whose character and conduct are to be accepted as infallible, but whose thoughts and convictions in regard to God and the soul and the future life are mere fallacies and illusions.

What does it mean to preach Christ?

Preach Christ, if it is to be a true watchword for our ministry to the present age, must be cleared and vivified and expanded in our consciousness. We must know what we mean by it, and we must try to know what we ought to mean. We must ask ourselves again and again whether the thing that we do mean is always quite, or even approximately, the thing that we ought to mean when we use this precious and powerful phrase. It was commonly employed, say fifty years ago, to describe by way of distinction a presentation of Jesus which dwelt chiefly or entirely upon His death as the vicarious sacrifice for sin. It is frequently employed now as if it meant little or nothing more than the graphic description of Christ's life and actions as the supreme type of virtue and love. But surely to preach Christ exclusively in either of these ways is to divide Him. It is not enough to have a Christocentric theology. It is not enough to have a Christocentric morality. We must not only put Him at the centre; but we must also draw the circumference so that it shall embrace the whole of human life.

If Christ is the Lamb of God that taketh away the sin of the world,[1] He is also the true Light which lighteth every man that cometh into the world.[2] If He is the fulfilment of all dim prophecies of good, He is also the head and source of a new unfolding of spiritual vision. If He is the way and the life, He is also the truth.[3] If He is immortal love, regenerating

A gospel for the whole circle of human life.

[1] St. John i. 29.   [2] St. John i. 9.   [3] St. John xiv. 6.

the affections, He is also immortal wisdom re-
organizing the thoughts, and immortal power
strengthening the wills, of men. If His heart
is to be the norm of our feeling, His mind is
to be the norm of our thinking. If He is the
herald and founder of a new and celestial
dominion upon earth, He is also the source of
authority in the kingdom of heaven.

I

The king-
dom of
heaven the
keynote of
Christ's
teaching.

The idea of the kingdom of heaven, as an actual reign of God over living men, in which all
ancient anticipations of good are accomplished
and a new state of virtue and blessedness is established on earth, was foremost and dominant
in the teaching of Jesus.[1] It was the keynote
of His ministry. Everything that He said,
everything that He did, was in harmony with
this master thought.

It is passing strange to see how often and
how utterly this keynote has been changed in
the variations which men have woven about the

[1] The word "kingdom" is used in the Gospels more than
a hundred times to express the new condition of human life
which Christ came to announce and establish. In St.
Matthew's Gospel the favourite phrase is "the kingdom of
heaven." St. Mark and St. Luke use "the kingdom of
God."

original theme of Christianity; and how far *False inter-*
we are, even yet, from hearing it clearly, and *pretations.*
sounding it with dominant fulness, in the
music of religion. At times the kingdom of
heaven has been identified with the visible
church as an outward embodiment of power in
the world. And surely this interpretation is
far enough away from the thought of Christ,
who taught expressly that the kingdom was
invisible and inward. At other times men have
removed their conception from the present to
the future, and looked for its realization in the
life of the redeemed after death, or in the second
coming of Christ to reign in millennial glory.
And surely this interpretation is equally remote
from Christ's teaching, at the very outset of His
ministry and all through its course, that the
kingdom of heaven was at hand, that it had
already come near to men, and was lying all
around them, close to them, pressing upon them
from every side so that many were already entering into it and dwelling within it.

The unreality and incompleteness of these *The idea*
two opposite interpretations of the kingdom *almost lost*
produced their natural results. The idea fell
out of its true place in Christian thought. It
became obscure, subordinate, and was finally

almost obliterated. No further illustration of this statement is necessary than that which may be obtained by consulting one of the most popular aids to the study of the Bible : Talbot's *Analysis*, revised by the Rev. Nathaniel West, and again revised by the Rev. Dr. Roswell D. Hitchcock, and set forth under the title of *A Complete Analysis of the Holy Bible; or, the Whole Bible arranged in Subjects*.[1] In the index to this work there is but one solitary reference to the kingdom of God. When we turn to look at it, we find eleven verses, under the heading of " The Millennium ; the Growth of the Kingdom of God." The kingdom of heaven is dismissed with a general reference to the Parables. To any one who is really familiar with his New Testament, the insufficiency of such a treatment of one of its controlling ideas must appear evident and surprising.

The idea begins to be restored.

But it may be said that in very recent times there has been an intense revival of interest in this idea and an immense amount of good work done in the study and explication of it. This is true and it should be gratefully recognized. Such books as those which Dr. James S. Candlish and Professor A. B. Bruce have written

[1] Wilmore's *New Analytical Reference Bible* (New York, 1891).

upon "The Kingdom of God," are most valuable gifts to Christian literature.[1] And yet I will frankly confess that these books, and others like them, seem to me rather to point the way than to reach the goal. The fulness of the conception of the kingdom of heaven is not yet restored in current theology. Its regnancy in all spheres of human life is not yet completely rounded. There is still a great deal of work to be done in this direction by the Christian thinker and the Christian preacher. The vision of the kingdom is obscured, the proclamation of the kingdom is weakened, because it is still presented too exclusively as a kingdom of grace, and not with equal emphasis as a kingdom of truth : it is set up too partially as a standard for the character and conduct of men, and not with equal clearness as a standard for their thoughts and convictions.

One reason of this one-sidedness, it seems to me, lies in the fact that we have hitherto been looking almost entirely to the first three Gospels as the source of our knowledge of the true

It must be studied in all four Gospels.

[1] *The Kingdom of God, Biblically and Historically Considered*, James S. Candlish (Edinburgh, Clarks, 1884). *The Kingdom of God, or Christ's Teaching according to the Synoptical Gospels*, Alexander Balmain Bruce (New York, Scribners, 1889).

N

meaning of the kingdom of heaven. But the
Fourth Gospel, if indeed it be, as the best
modern scholars say it is, "the most faithful
image and memorial of Jesus that any man
could produce," must be no less important, no
less significant in the light which it throws
upon this controlling idea of His mind. And
when we turn to study it with this aim in view,
we find at once that it gives us what we need.
It completes and rounds out the record of the
three other Gospels. It answers the questions which they suggest. It keeps the promises which they seem to make to our faith.
And it is only when we take the fourfold
narrative in its entirety that we begin to catch
sight of the satisfying and convincing fulness
of the idea of the kingdom of heaven.

The king-
dom in
St. John.

This idea underlies the whole Gospel according to St. John. It is no less fundamental, no
less necessary here than it is in the Synoptic
Gospels. It is presented in different forms,
because the type of the writer's mind and the
purpose of his book are different. But it is
the same idea. And this presentation of it is
essential to its completeness.

In the Synoptics we have the conditions of
entrance into the kingdom, a child-like spirit,[1]

[1] St. Matt. xviii. 3.

faith,[1] repentance,[2] and obedience.[3]   In St. John *Compared with the Synoptics* we have the spiritual birth by which alone those requisites are made possible.[4]   In the Synoptics we have the laws of the kingdom.[5] In St. John we have the new life in which alone those laws can be fulfilled.[6]   In the Synoptics we have the parables and pictures of the kingdom.[7]   In St. John we have the inmost sense of those parables, spoken directly to the soul, in words of which Christ Himself says "they are spirit, and they are life."[8]   In the Synoptics we have the new order of human society in the imitation by the disciples of Christ's obedience to the will of God.[9]   In St. John we have the organizing principle of that new order in Christ's revelation of Himself to the disciples as the way, the truth, and the life.[10]   In the Synoptics we have the supremacy of Christ's example over men's hearts.   In St. John we have the supremacy of Christ's teachings over men's minds.

Of course, I do not mean to say that either

[1] St. Matt. ix. 22 ; St. Mark x. 52.
[2] St. Luke xiii. 3.
[3] St. Matt. v. 20.
[4] St. John iii. 5.
[5] The Sermon on the Mount.
[6] St. John vi. 22–65.
[7] St. Matt. xiii., xxi., xxv.; St. Luke xiii., xvii., xix., etc.
[8] St. John vi. 63; viii. 12–51.
[9] St. Matt. xii. 50.
[10] St. John xiv. 6.

Both views necessary.

of these aspects of the kingdom is confined exclusively to the source in which it is most fully and clearly exhibited.[1] But this is what I mean. The Synoptics give us the first and simplest description of the nature of the kingdom. St. John gives us the fullest and clearest revelation of the mind of the King. We cannot understand the former without the latter. We cannot enter into the full meaning of the initial proclamation of Jesus, when He walked beside the Sea of Galilee crying "The kingdom of heaven has come near,"[2] unless we go on with Him to the judgment-hall, and hear Him give His final answer to Pilate : "Thou sayest that I am a King; to this end have I been born, and to this end am I come into the world, that I should bear witness unto the truth ; every one that is of the truth heareth my voice."[3]

When we stand at this point, when we accept this declaration as the key to unlock and open the inmost meaning of the manifestation of the Father in the human life of the Son, we

[1] See Bruce, *The Kingdom of God*, p. 185, on the personal claim of Christ in the Synoptics. See R. F. Horton, *The Teaching of Jesus* (New York, 1896), pp. 219–233, on relation between Synoptic doctrine of the kingdom and Johannine doctrine of eternal life.

[2] St. Matt. iv. 17.   [3] St. John xviii. 37.

begin to apprehend the inexhaustible scope and *The king-dom of truth as well as of grace.* significance of our call to preach Christ to an age of doubt. It is a gospel not only for the affections, but also for the intellect. It takes up His words as well as His works and makes them vital in the lives of men. It conceives and proclaims the kingdom of heaven as something more than "the reign of divine love exercised by God in His grace over human hearts believing in His love and constrained thereby to yield Him grateful affection and devoted service."[1] It is also the reign of divine truth exercised through a faithful witness over the minds of men who submit to His guidance and are led by Him into inward peace and unity of thought. And the source of authority in this kingdom of heaven, which is equally a realm of truth and a realm of grace, is Jesus the Christ, whose doctrine, as well as His example, is ultimate and supreme.

II

Let us observe in passing that we have precisely the same basis to rest upon in our preaching of the doctrine of Jesus as in our preaching of His character and life. If historical criticism *The King as a teacher.*

[1] Bruce, *The Kingdom of God*, p. 46.

gives us good reason to believe, as all candid
inquirers now admit, that the four Gospels contain a veritable picture of an actual personage
who once lived on earth, there is equally good
reason to believe that they have preserved for
us a trustworthy account of His teaching in its
substance and spirit. If we can justly claim

*The doctrine
of Christ.*
that His character is so perfect and transcendent that no man of that age, however gifted or
learned, and least of all such men as the writers
of the New Testament, could possibly have invented it; we can make the same claim, with
equal justice, for the body of doctrine which
is attributed to Christ. In its coherence, its
clarity, its sublimity, and its universality it
altogether surpasses the mental abilities and
the religious insight of the writers of the four
Gospels. Indeed, it is frankly confessed that
the disciples of Jesus were so far from being
able to invent His doctrine, that they actually
misunderstood and misinterpreted many of its
truths when they first heard them. It was
contrary to their prejudices and expectations.
They did not put it into His mouth. He revealed it to their minds. Their faith in it
rested upon His personal authority. And it
was only as they kept company with Him
and followed Him, receiving His word into

their souls and translating it into their lives, that it became to them luminous and satisfying and convincing.

We are entitled, or rather we are compelled, to regard the teaching of Jesus as an objective fact just as much as His life and character. The record of it bears on its face the overwhelming evidence of verity. All the results of literary criticism are squarely against the supposition that such a doctrine as that which is presented to us under His name in the four Gospels, could ever have been pieced together out of the thoughts and imaginations of widely separated and divergent minds, and attributed to an unknown and perhaps mythical Master. It is not a mosaic; it is a living unity. It is not a creation of faith; it is the creator of faith. The hypothesis that four men agreed, or happened, to gather together out of the Hebrew prophets, and the heathen philosophers, and the mysterious and inexplicable inner consciousness of the new-born Christian churches, certain beautiful ideas in regard to God and the soul and the future life, and ascribe them to Jesus, utterly breaks down at the touch of reality. The central, unifying, formative quality of the teaching of Christ is the one thing that

An objective reality.

is most evident in the record.   It is emphasized by all the phenomena of growth, of vital
development, of deepening power, which may
be traced from the sermon in the synagogue
at Nazareth to the discourse in the upper room
at Jerusalem.   It shines out unmistakably
through all the living variety of impressions
which it made upon various minds, and
through all the consequent many-sidedness of
the report which is given of it.   Not more
certainly did the character of Christ inspire
and unite the lives of His followers than
His doctrine illuminated and controlled their
beliefs.   The only view which meets the facts
is that Jesus really lived, and really taught.
thus and so, as He is presented to us in the
Gospels.

*The form of
the record.*
This brings us at once to the most important
feature in the record of His teaching.   It is not
given to us in the form of an abstract system,
a treatise on theology, or a summary of doctrine, written down by the hand of Jesus.   He
Himself made no record of His words.   Only
once do we see Him writing, — in the beautiful
episode which a later tradition has added to the
eighth chapter of St. John's Gospel.   Historical or not, the incident is profoundly sugges-
tive.   For Jesus wrote not with a pen upon

enduring parchment, nor with a stylus upon imperishable brass :

> " He stooped
> And wrote upon *the unrecording ground.*" [1]

He would not leave even a single line of manuscript where His followers could preserve it with literal reverence and worship it as a sacred relic. He chose to inscribe His teaching upon no other leaves than those which are folded within the human soul. He chose to trust His words to the faithful keeping of memory and love ; and He said of them, with sublime confidence, that they should never pass away.[2] He chose that the truth which He declared and the life which He lived should never be divided, but that they should go down together through the ages.

And this is precisely what has come to pass. The Church in past ages has often been inclined to abstract the doctrines of Christianity concerning the person and work of Christ from their union with His human life, and to condense them into a purely formal system of dogma for the intellect. The Church in the present age shows at least a tendency to separate the image

Inseparable from His character.

---

[1] Katrina Trask, " A Night and Morning in Jerusalem " (*Harper's Magazine*, April, 1896).

[2] St. Mark xiii. 31.

of Jesus from the truths which He taught, and hold Him up to men merely as an ideal of holiness and goodness. But the one barrier that stands firm against both these false tendencies is the marvellous narrative of the Gospels, in which the life and the doctrine of Christ are woven together, one and inseparable, like a robe without seam.

Words and life interpret each other.

How can we understand His grace, unless we accept His truth ? How can we appreciate His truth, unless we receive His grace ? At every step, His action is interpreted and explained by His words. He trusts in Providence, and He commands His disciples to trust, not merely because submissive confidence is a beautiful and happy thing, but because He knows and declares that God is really a Father, worthy to be trusted.[1] He prays, secretly and openly; secretly because He is sure that God hears Him always, and openly because He would fain give this assurance to others.[2] He seeks the sinful and the lost, not merely because such a ministry is lovely and gracious, but because He knows and declares that it is the will of God, and that there is more joy in heaven over one sinner that repenteth than over ninety-and-nine just

[1] St. Matt. vi. 25–30.   [2] St. John xi. 41, 42.

men that need no repentance.[1] He cares for
the bodies of men and He relieves their wants,
but He cares infinitely more for their souls and
He teaches them to care more, because He
knows that the soul is capable of immortality
and more precious than all that this world can
give.[2] He moves willingly and obediently to
the cross, not because it is inevitable, not because resignation is the crown of virtue, but
because He knows and declares that this is the
sacrifice appointed for Him as the Christ, the
laying down of His life as a ransom for many,
the lifting up by which He is to draw all men
unto Himself.[3] He goes down into death with
unshaken courage, not because it is a fine thing
to be brave, but because He knows and declares
that He is returning to the Father and that He
will bring those who love Him to be with Him
where He is forever.[4]

Now these are declarations of great truths.
If we deny them, if we make them uncertain,
the life which was built upon them has no
meaning, no substance, no power in it. It becomes a splendid illusion, a heroic mistake.

The doctrine of Christ the basis of His conduct.

[1] St. Luke xv. 7.
[2] St. John vi. 27; St. Mark viii. 36, 37.
[3] St. Mark ix 12 ; St. Matt. xx. 28; St. John xii. 32.
[4] St. John xiv. 1–3.

But if we accept them, then, and only then, that life becomes the rock of our confidence, the substance of things hoped for and the evidence of things not seen.[1] For it was on the knowledge of these things that Jesus actually founded His own character and His conduct. It was by believing thus and so, and by living up to His belief, that He was made perfect. And it was by teaching His disciples to believe thus and so that He would bind them to follow His example and inspire them to share His life. "Whosoever heareth these sayings of mine and doeth them, I will liken him unto a wise man which built his house upon a rock."[2] "Now ye are clean through the word which I have spoken unto you." "If ye abide in me, and my words abide in you, ye shall ask what ye will and it shall be done unto you."[3]

---

[1] "Nicht das Leben Jesu an sich in seinem geschichtlichen Verlaufe, sondern die Auffassung der religiosen Bedeutung desselben, auf welche die älteste N. T. liche Verkundigung ruht, bildet den Ausgangspunkt fur die biblische Theologie. Diese Auffassung war aber zunächst bedingt durch die Lehre Jesu, sofern dieselbe die authentische Erlauterung über die Bedeutung seiner Person und seiner Erscheinung gab, und daher muss eine Darstellung dieser Lehre den grundlegenden Abschnitt der biblischen Theologie bilden." — BERNHARD WEISS, *Lehrbuch der Biblischen Theologie des Neuen Testaments* (2te Auflage, Berlin, 1873), p. 31.

[2] St. Matt. vii. 24.   [3] St. John xv. 3, 7.

III

The importance which Christ ascribed to His words as the authoritative revelation of unseen verities to the confused and darkened minds of men, cannot be denied or overlooked by any one who reads the Gospels candidly and intelligently. It is true, indeed, that He expressly disclaimed the idea that His doctrine was created, or invented, or even discovered by Himself. He said, "My doctrine is not mine but His that sent me,"[1] "All things that I have heard of my Father I have made known unto you."[2] But it is equally true that He claimed an absolute infallibility for the message which was revealed in Him, committed unto Him, and delivered by Him. This claim is made with equal force in the Synoptics and in St. John. "No one knoweth who the Son is, save the Father; and who the Father is, save the Son, and he to whomsoever the Son willeth to reveal Him."[3] "We speak that we do know, and bear witness of that we have seen."[4] This is not the language that an honest and conscientious teacher would use to describe his religious opinions or his spiritual

The authority of Christ's teaching.

---

[1] St. John vii. 16.   [3] St. Luke x. 22.
[2] St. John xv. 15.   [4] St. John iii. 11.

hopes.   The wisest and the best of men have always hesitated to assume this tone of certainty in regard to their deepest reflections upon the mysteries of being.   But from first to last this tone marks the teaching of Jesus. "They were astonished at His teaching; for He taught them as having authority, and not as the scribes."[1]

It is original.

It is evident that He intended to speak thus. For nothing is more striking in the manner of His teaching than the absence of all reliance upon corroborative testimony or traditional support.[2]   He did not seek to defend His positions with a formidable array of great names. He did not make a long catena of quotations from learned sources.   He gave out His doctrine from the depth of His own consciousness as a flower breathes perfume, fresh, pure, original, and convincing.   He certainly felt a Divine inspiration in the ancient Hebrew Scriptures. The law and the prophets conveyed to Him the

[1] St. Mark i. 22.

[2] " Avec une certitude sereine, qui ne semble pas terrestre, il disait ces choses.   Il chantait, comme aucun prophète n'avait su le faire, le chant des revoirs éternels qui a bercé pendant des siècles les souffrances et les agonies.   Et ce chant-là, voici que de nos jours, au triste déclin des temps, les hommes se meurent de ne plus l'entendre." — PIERRE LOTI, *La Galilée* (Paris, 1896), p. 94.

word of God. He used them on certain occasions to repel the assaults of evil, as in the temptation in the wilderness. He used them on other occasions to convince and convict the Scribes and Pharisees out of their own Scriptures. But He never rested upon them as the sole and sufficient basis of His doctrine. He was not a commentator on truths already revealed. He *A new revelation.* was a revealer of new truth. His teaching was not the exposition; it was the text. And this higher revelation not only fulfilled, but also surpassed, the old; replacing the temporal by the eternal, the figurative by the factual, the literal by the spiritual, the imperfect by the perfect. How often Jesus quoted from the Old Testament in order to show that it was already old and insufficient; that its forms of speech and rules of conduct were like the husk of the seed which must be shattered by the emergence of the living germ. His doctrine was in fact a moral and intellectual daybreak for the world. He did far more than supply a novel system of conduction for an ancient light. He sent forth from Himself a new illumination, transcending all that had gone before, as the sunrise overfloods the pale glimmering of the morning star set like a beacon of promise upon the coast of dawn.

It is self-evidencing.

He did not rely upon reasoning for the proof of His doctrine. He put no trust in the compulsion of logic, in the keenness of dialectics. We look in vain among His words for an exhibition of the "evidences of Christianity." He did not endeavour to demonstrate the existence of God or the immortality of the soul. What He said was meant to be its own evidence. His method was not apologetic; it was declaratory.

"He argued not, but preached, and conscience did the rest."

The result of this is marvellous and magnificent. His teaching is cleared and disentangled from all that is temporary and transient in human thought. If He had reasoned with men, it must have been done upon the premisses and in the forms of philosophy current in that age. Otherwise He could not have reached their intelligence, His reasoning would have been of none effect. But because He passed by all these processes and left them on one side while His doctrine moved simply, directly, and majestically to the heart of the truth, it comes to us to-day free and unencumbered by any of those theories of physical science, of psychology, of political economy, which the growth of knowledge has changed, discredited,

or discarded. His teaching is neither ancient *It is uni-*
nor modern, neither deductive nor inductive, *versal.*
neither Jewish nor Greek. It is universal,
enduring, valid for all minds and for all times.
There are no more difficulties in the way of
accepting it now than there were when it was
first delivered. It fits the spiritual needs of
the nineteenth, as closely as it fitted the
spiritual needs of the first, century. It carries the same attractions, the same credentials
in the Western Hemisphere as it carried in
the Eastern. It stands out as clearly from all
the later, as it did from all the earlier, philosophies. It finds the soul as inevitably to-day
as it did at first. And the men of this age
who hear Christ can only say, as His disciples
said long ago, "Lord, to whom shall we go?
Thou hast the words of eternal life." [1]

And yet how few are those words, compared *It is small*
with the utterances of other teachers. How *in compass.*
small in compass is the doctrine of Jesus as it
has come down to us. Eighty pages of a duo-
decimo book will hold all of His recorded discourses and the story of His life. Other words
He must have spoken while He was on earth,
but I doubt not that they moved within the
same circle. For even in the present record

[1] St. John vi. 68.

o

we find the same truths recurring again and again, expressed in different language, arranged in different sequence, as the evangelists retrace, each from his own point of view, the memory of the things which Jesus taught to the multitudes and to His disciples. The literature of the world holds no other doctrine so limited in bulk, so limitless in meaning.

Its fontal quality.

The teaching of Christ differs from that of all other masters in its fontal quality. It is comprised in a little space, but it has an infinite fulness. Its utterance is closely bounded, but its significance is inexhaustible. The sacred books of other religions, the commentaries and expositions on the Christian religion, spread before us a vast and intricate expanse, like lakes of truth mixed with error, stretching away into the distance, arm after arm, bay after bay, until we despair of being able even to explore their coasts and trace their windings. When we come back to Christ, we find, not an inland sea of doctrine, but a clear fountain of living water, springing up into everlasting life.

An unfailing source.

Calm, pure, unfathomable, it is never clouded and it never fails. The inspiration of other teachers rises and falls like an intermittent spring. To-day it is brimming full; to-mor-

row it is empty and dry. But the truth that
flows from Jesus is constant and unvarying.
The Spirit always rests upon Him. The
Father is always with Him. Out of the deep
serenity of His soul, as from some secret vale
of peace high among the eternal hills, the vital
spring of truth wells up forever, and forever
the crystal stream runs down to refresh and
revive the souls of men.

New meanings come out of the teaching of *Always renewed.*
Jesus in every land and in every age. New
stars are mirrored in its depths. New flowers
blossom on its banks. New fields of love are
fertilized by its waters. It is not that each
succeeding century and race adds something of
its own to the doctrine of Christ. It is that
each finds in that source something which was
meant to become its own, and so to satisfy its
deepest needs. The old questions are repeated
in new words, and the new answer comes in the
old words.[1] The truth as it is in Jesus does
not have to be changed and adapted to fit it for
a world-wide missionary enterprise. It needs
only to be purified from the things that men

[1] " Socrates asked questions which his disciples tried to
answer ; Jesus provoked His disciples to ask questions which
He answered."— JAMES STALKER, *Imago Christi* (New York,
Armstrongs, 1889), p. 270.

have mingled with it, restored to the simplicity that is in Christ, and it proves itself as fresh, as satisfying, as life-bestowing to the thirsty soul in America or in the islands of the sea, as it did in Galilee or on the hillsides of Judea.

The sim-
plicity that
is in Christ.

When we ask ourselves why it is that the doctrine of the Master has this enduring, self-renewing, fontal character, I think we must find the answer in the fact that it simply bears witness, with a directness and inevitableness altogether unparalleled, to the actual existence of a spiritual world corresponding to the spiritual faculties and aspirations of men. It does not turn aside to discuss metaphysical problems or theological subtleties. The distinction between the natural and the supernatural does not even appear in the teaching of Jesus. There may, or there may not, be such a distinction. If there is, He at least does not think it important enough to speak of it. The one thing of which He wishes to make men sure is that the same God who sends His sunshine and His rain upon the evil and upon the good, the same God whose bounty feeds the birds of the air and clothes the lilies of the field with beauty, hears in secret the prayers of the penitent and believing and rewards them openly. The question of the how and the where of the life after death

is not even touched in the teaching of Jesus.
It matters little. The one thing that He declares with unfaltering certainty is the reality
of that life. The one thing that He presses
home upon the minds of men with calm intensity is the danger of losing it through sin and
unbelief. The one thing that He tenderly and
urgently pleads with them to do, is to make
sure of its immortal blessedness through faith
and love and obedience to Him. And so, at
every point, He passes by the non-essential to
touch the essential, He disregards the passing
curiosity to satisfy the real anxiety, He neglects
the shadows to reveal the substance of the
unseen world.

Teaching like this is the only kind of teaching that will always renew itself, always have
something more to bestow upon us. It cannot
grow obsolete. It cannot be drained of its significance. It is like life. Nay, it is life, and it
gives life.

Words of eternal life.

IV

Let us understand, then, that if our Christianity is to satisfy our whole nature, if it is to
have its real and full meaning, and power to
bring in the kingdom of heaven, it must include this element. We must be as loyal to

Loyalty to Christ's teaching.

the teaching of Jesus as we are to His example.
We must count no pains too great to spend
upon the study of that teaching as it lies in
the records, and no effort too severe to make
in order that it may be restored in its integrity and entirety, rounded and harmonized,
within the very centre of our minds. And
then we must preach it, simply, sincerely, certainly, as the only doctrine which can lead
men out of the intellectual anarchy of doubt
into the peaceful realm of truth.

The age demands authority.

This is what the age is looking and longing
for. It can find no joy in the kingdom of
heaven unless it finds there a source of authority for the mind as well as for the heart. Authority is what the sociologist demands, in order
that he may have a sure basis for the precepts
of altruism. Authority is what the philosopher
seeks, in order that he may have a fixed point
of departure and certain limits of speculation.
Authority is what the poet craves, as he clings
to

> " The truths that never can be *proved*,
> Until we close with all we loved
> And all we flow from, soul in soul." [1]

Men are crying lo here ! and lo there ! We
must find the source of authority in an in-

[1] Tennyson, *In Memoriam*.

errant Book, or in an enlightened reason, or in an infallible Church, or perhaps in all three; as if there could be three sources of one authority, or as if a channel could ever be rightly called a source! Let us not hesitate to pass through this confusion of tongues and of ideas, serene and untroubled, with the message of a more excellent way.

Christ is the Light of all Scripture. Christ is the Master of holy reason. Christ is the sole Lord and Life of the true Church. By His word we test all doctrines, conclusions, and commands. On His word we build all faith. This is *the* source of authority in the kingdom of heaven. Let us neither forget nor hesitate to appeal to it always with untrembling certainty and positive conviction. If Christ did not know and preach the truth, then there is no truth that can be known or preached. Unless we are sure of this, we would better go out of business entirely. It is inconceivable that the loftiest character in history should be the most mistaken man that ever thought about the real basis and meaning of life. It is incredible that the noblest life in the world should be founded upon a faith that was vain. It is impossible that a supreme devotion and a real likeness to Christ should

Christ is the supreme authority.

have been produced and perpetuated in the world without a veritable apprehension of that which He knew and taught concerning God and man.

Our great task, to learn His creed.

To have this apprehension clearly formed within us must be our ardent and joyful intellectual endeavour. We are not to rest content with the study of single words and separate phrases. The limitations of language, the conditions of transmission, will always expose us to error if we follow that course. The truth as it is in Jesus does not lie in fragments, but in the rounded whole. We must get back to the unity and integrity of the thoughts of Jesus, the creed of Christ. The broad outline of His vision of things human and divine, the central verities which appear firm and unchangeable in all the reports of His teaching, the point of view from which He discerned and interpreted the mystery of life, — that is what we must seek. And when we find it, we must take our stand there as men who feel the solid ground beneath their feet. Illustrations and confirmations we may gather from science and history and philosophy. But the rock of certainty is the mind of Jesus, expressed in His living words and in His speak-

ing life. Beyond this we need not and we
cannot go. Here is the ultimatum. This is
the truth, we say to men, because Jesus knew
it, and said it, and lived it.

But one thing we may not, we dare not, forget. The condition of apprehending, and how
much more of preaching, the truth revealed by
Christ is that we abide in Him. The word of
Jesus in the mind of one who does not do the
will of Jesus, lies like seed-corn in a mummy's
hand. It is only by dwelling with Him and
receiving His character, His personality so
profoundly, so vitally that it shall be with us
as if, in His own words, we had partaken of
His flesh and His blood, as if His sacred
humanity had been interwoven with the very
fibres of our heart and pulsed with secret power
in all our veins, — it is thus only that we can
be enabled to see His teaching as it is, and set
it forth with luminous conviction to the souls
of men.

We must live in Him to know His doctrine.

And if ever we ourselves become afraid of
our own task, and shrink from it ; if the scepticism of our age appalls us and chills us to the
very marrow ; if we question whether a gospel
so simple, so absolute, as that which is committed to us can find acceptance in such a
world, at such a time as this, — be sure it is

Return to Jesus.

because we have gotten out of fellowship with Him who is our Peace and our Hope, our Light and our Strength. A Christless man can never preach Christ. We have been anxious and troubled about many things, and have forgotten the one thing needful. Peace we must have before we can have power. Let us straightway return, in prayer, in meditation, in trust, in faithful simple-hearted obedience, to Him who is the only centre of Peace because He is the only source of authority.

> " I have a life in Christ to live,
>   But ere I live it must I wait
> Till learning can clear answer give
>   Of this and that book's date?
> I have a life in Christ to live,
>   I have a death in Christ to die; —
> And must I wait till science give
>   All doubts a full reply?
>
> Nay, rather, while the sea of doubt
> Is raging wildly round about,
> Questioning of life and death and sin,
> Let me but creep within
> Thy fold, O Christ, and at Thy feet
> Take but the lowest seat,
> And hear Thine awful voice repeat
> In gentlest accents, heavenly sweet,
> Come unto Me and rest;
> Believe Me, and be blest." [1]

[1] John Campbell Shairp.

VI

LIBERTY

" But, perfect in every part,
    Has the potter's moulded shape
Leap of man's quickened heart,
    Throe of his thought's escape,
Stings of his soul which dart

" Through the barrier of flesh, till keen
    She climbs from the calm and clear
Through turbidity all between
    From the known to the unknown here,
Heaven's ' Shall be,' from Earth's ' Has been ' ?

" Then life is — to wake and not sleep,
    Rise and not rest, but press
From earth's level where blindly creep
    Things perfected, more or less,
To the heaven's height, far and steep,

" Where, amid what strifes and storms
    May wait the adventurous quest,
Power is Love — transports, transforms
    Who aspired from worst to best,
Sought the soul's world, spurned the worms.' "

— ROBERT BROWNING, *Reverie.*

VI

LIBERTY

THERE are three points at which the teaching of Jesus comes into closest contact with the needs of the present age. Three problems of profound difficulty are pressing to-day upon all thoughtful men: the psychological problem of the freedom of the will; the theological problem of the actual relation of God to the universe ; and the moral problem of man's duty to his fellow-men in a world of inequality. Out of the depths of these problems dark and multitudinous doubts are forever rising, like the clouds of smoke and steam which issue from the labouring bosom of Vesuvius, while subterranean thunder is muttering and rolling underneath. Most of the intellectual perplexities and practical perils of our times come directly from these questions, to which modern scepticism gives an answer of despair, or at best only a dubious and uncertain reply.

Three great problems.

But the gospel of Christ, rightly apprehended and interpreted, offers us a solution

205

of these problems which is full of light and hope and moral certainty. There is a breath of the Spirit in His teaching, pure and strong, pouring like a clean wind out of heaven, to scoff away the obscuring vapours, and reveal the changeless verities and glories of the spiritual landscape. Three truths emerge in His doctrine, and stand out clear and sharp as mountain peaks against the blue : the truth of human liberty, the truth of Divine sovereignty, and the truth of universal service. Of these three truths we must never lose sight, if our thinking is to be in accordance with the mind of Jesus. To these three truths we must bear witness, unhesitatingly, faithfully, and joyfully, if our preaching is to be a gospel for this age of doubt.

I

No one who has looked steadily upon the face of modern life as it is reflected in popular literature can doubt that it is "sicklied o'er" with the dark shadow of fatalism. It is evident in the writings of the learned and in the scribblings of the ignorant. Everywhere there is a tendency to explain the whole life of man as the product of heredity and environment. The student of physiology, tracing the strange and subtle correspondence between the processes of consciousness and the changes and movements of the nervous system, makes the enormous assumption that the correspondence amounts to identity. All the hopes and fears, all the affections and aspirations, which glorify this mortal life, are in their last analysis the result of certain puckerings and tintinnabulations of the gray matter of the nerves. The actions which flow from them are as necessary as the fall of an apple when the stem is broken. The caress which a mother gives to her child, and the blow with which a murderer strikes his victim dead, are equally automatic and inevitable. They are the motions of delicately constructed puppets, and the triumph of modern investigation is the discovery of the string which moves them and the forces which pull it.

It is true that many of the teachers who steer us, more or less openly, towards this conclusion are careful to disavow the idea that they are teaching materialism. The name is highly unpopular at the present moment, and there is hardly one of the men of science of to-day who has not protested with indignation that no one should dare to call him a materialist. They have devised subtle theories of something called "mind-stuff" which they hold,

Materialism disavowed but taught.

with W. K. Clifford, "is the reality which we perceive as matter." They distinguish, with Huxley, between matter and force, and a third thing which they call consciousness and which they admit cannot conceivably be a modification of either of the first two things ; but they go on to say that "what we call the operations of the mind are functions of the brain, and the materials of consciousness are products of cerebral activity." [1] In short, they give a materialistic explanation of the origin and processes of thought, and then protect themselves against the imputation of being materialists, by solemnly averring that they have not the slightest idea of what matter really is, nor the slightest intention of suggesting that it has any resemblance to the so-called mental operations which are probably produced by one of its own forms of activity.

Responsibility crowded out.

A scheme like this certainly has no room for free-will or personal responsibility. It makes a man's character and action entirely dependent upon the amount and quality of nervous energy that has been transmitted to him by his ancestors and developed by the circumstances of his life. He lives, as Professor Tyndall

[1] T. H. Huxley, in *The Fortnightly Review*, vol. xi., 793.

says, in a realm of "physical and moral necessity," — though why he should be at pains to
say "moral," I can hardly conceive. One ad-
jective would serve as well as two, when they
both mean the same thing. It requires but
a little exercise of this nervous energy on our
part, in the form of imagination, to trace it back
to its previous form of heat stored up in certain hundredweights of food and appropriated
by digestion. From this point our cerebral
activity skips lightly and altogether without
volition along the various lines of animal and
vegetable life, of chemical and physical trans-
formations of energy, until we arrive at the
idea of the sun. From this idea a certain un-
controllable change in the gray substance of
our brain produces the further notion that
the arrangement of certain quantities of matter and force which took place in some inexplicable way long before the birth of the
solar system was really the thing that settled
the question whether you and I should prefer
telling the truth to lying, — if we do. Indeed,
there never has been any question at all about
it; it was fixed from the beginning. We have
no more responsibility for it than we have for
the colour of our eyes or the shape of our
noses.

P

I have found a brief and explicit statement of the position to which this method of thinking forces those who follow it, in an article ironically entitled " Thoughts of a Human Automaton " in a recent English periodical.[1]

" I am an automaton — a puppet dangling on my distinctive wire, which Fate holds with an unrelaxing grip. I am not different, nor do I feel differently, from my fellow-men, but my eyes refuse to blink away the truth, which is, that I am an automatic machine, a piece of clockwork wound up to go for an allotted time, smoothly or otherwise, as the efficiency of the machinery may determine. Free-will is a myth invented by man to satisfy his emotions, not his reason. I feel as if I were free, as if I were responsible for my thoughts and actions, just as a person under the influence of hypnotism believes he is free to do as he pleases. But he is not ; nor am I. If it were once possible for a rational being to question this fact, the discoveries of Darwin must have set his doubts at rest. . . .

" What is crime ? A crime is an action threatened by the law with punishment, says Kant ; and freedom of action or free-will

[1] Henry Beauchamp, in *The Fortnightly Review*, English edition, March, 1892.

is a legally necessary condition of crime. But the law of heredity conclusively demonstrates that free-will and freedom of action stand in the category of lively imaginings. Therefore crime, as the law understands it, is non-existent, since no imputability can be recognized when a man is not responsible for his actions. Therefore the law is not justified in inflicting punishment. . . .

" Briefly to conclude. Religion can no more mix with science than oil with water. Science acknowledges no necessity for the existence of religion, and finally severs the bonds between morality and religion. Morality, altogether independent of religion, is entirely based upon self-interest. The supposed connection between religion and morality is an illusion most pernicious to the general welfare and advance of mankind. Religion, as a superfluity, should be excluded from all educational institutions. Its place will be supplied by the creed of scientific philosophy — Determinism. The primary principle of Determinism, namely, that a human being is an automaton, and therefore not responsible for his thoughts or his acts, taken together with its corollaries, more than suffices for every intellectual need hitherto provided for by religion. For the two great factors in the value

of religion are its ethics and its sedative properties, and in both these uses Determinism
displays overwhelming intellectual superiority.
Its ethics are more universal and its consolation
more assured; for they both rest on irrefraga-
ble scientific truth. The Determinist is con-
sequently never harassed by doubts — the Rock
of Ages is fragile compared with the adaman-
tine foundation of his creed."

The creed of necessity. This curious claim of an automaton to have
a "creed" would be deliciously humorous, if
it were not so unutterably sad, and so detest-
ably dangerous. For though, as a matter of
fact, there are few men who will make, even
under an assumed name, such a candid confession of faith in their own moral non-entity
as that which we have just read, there are many
men who are, consciously or unconsciously,
preaching the same black creed of Necessity
in the subtle forms of literary art, and multitudes who are silently accepting it as gospel
truth. Fatalism broods over modern fiction
and the modern drama like a huge, shapeless
spectre; and its influence is felt in all the
judgments and conceptions and unspoken but
clearly revealed sentiments of a society which
finds its chief intellectual pabulum in novels
and plays.

Here is the famous French realist, Zola, of *"The Human Beast."* whose books it is said that enough have been sold to build a pile as high as the Eiffel tower. He writes a novel called *La Bête Humaine*, in which he shows how unswervingly the lines of evil run through the plan of life. He describes seven inevitable murders, occurring within eighteen months in close connection with a certain fated house, and closes his book with the description of a railway train, crowded with soldiers, dragged by an engine whose driver has been killed, dashing at headlong speed into the midnight. The train is the world; we are the freight; fate is the track; death is the darkness; God is the engineer, — who is dead.

Here is the leader of the Dutch Sensitivists, *"Footsteps of Fate."* Louis Couperus, who writes a romance called *Noodlot*, "*Destiny*," in which four human lives are tangled together in an inextricable and horrible coil. One of his characters pauses for an instant in the shameful career to which he is impelled. "He threw himself back in his chair, still feebly wringing his hands, and the tears trickled again and again down his cheeks. He saw his own cowardice take shape before him. He stared into its frightened eyes, and he did not condemn it. For he was as fate had made

him.   He was a craven, and he could not help
it.   Men called such an one as he a coward ; it
was but a word.   Why coward, or simple and
brave, or good and noble ?   It was all a matter
of convention, of accepted meaning ; the whole
world was mere convention, a concept, an illusion of the brain.   There was nothing real at
all — nothing ! " [1]

"Ghosts."

Here is the Norse dramatist, Ibsen, — the
new Shakespeare by the grace of heredity.   He
writes a drama of life which he calls *Ghosts*,
and shows how every player is haunted by dead
ancestors who look through his eyes, speak in
his words, and act in his deeds.   Echoes of
spent passion, shreds and patches of worn-out
sin, rags and tatters of the past, — that is the
stuff of which life is fabricated, like a piece of
shoddy cloth, in the great mill of circumstance
which stands on the banks of the river of time
and turns out the shabby lives of men and
women.

*The small
fatalists.*

Nor is this view of life confined to the great
foreign masters of realism.   It pervades almost
all the minor schools of fiction ; it diffuses itself insensibly through the work of the feeble
and fatuous imitators.   A keen and wholesome

---

[1] Louis Couperus, *The Footsteps of Fate* (New York,
Appletons), p. 65.

critic of our own literature, Mr. Charles Dudley Warner, put his finger upon the fact when he wrote : " It has come about that the novels and stories which are to fill our leisure hours and cheer us in this vale of tears have become what we call tragic. It is not easy to define what tragedy is, but the term is applied in modern fiction to scenes and characters that come to ruin from no particular fault of their own, — not even when the characters break most of the ten commandments, — but by an unappeasable fate that dogs and thwarts them. This is the romance of fatality, and if it is tragedy, it is the tragedy of fatalism."

It is not possible that such a theory of existence should prevail without bringing sadness and heaviness into the hearts of men. The modern melancholy of which we spoke in the first lecture is largely the result of this general sense of a godless predestination. It is Calvinism with the bottom knocked out. It robs life of all interest, of all joy, of all enthusiasm. Was it morphine that drove Guy de Maupassant, the most brilliant of the younger French novelists, to insanity? Or was it his philosophy that drove him to morphine as a refuge from the despair and ugliness of exist-

Melancholy marionettes

ence? Pessimism exudes from fatalism like sepia from the cuttlefish. What could be more dispiriting than to doubt the reality of all effort, to deny the possibility of self-conquest and triumph over circumstances, to find heroism an illusion and virtue a dream? What could break the spring of life more completely than to feel that our feet are tangled in a net whose meshes were woven for us by our ancestors, and for them by tailless apes, and for them by gilled amphibians, and for them by gliding worms, and for them by ciliated larvæ, and for them by amœbæ, and for them by God does not know what? It does not help the case in the least to do as some theologians have tried to do and bring back into the theory by the aid of certain misconstrued and very much overworked passages of Scripture, the idea of a supreme Deity who has constructed the loom and devised the pattern of the net and decreed the weaving of every loop. The chain of Fate is not made less heavy by fastening the end of it to the distant throne of an omnipotent and impassive Creator. If our false sense of freedom comes from such a Being, who is Himself free, it is all the more a cruel and bitter enigma. If moral responsibility has been imposed upon us by the same hand which has bound us to an inalterable destiny, it is all the more a crushing and miserable fraud. To baptize fatalism with a Christian name does not change its nature. To hold fast to the metaphysical conception of God while accepting Heredity and Environment as His only and infallible prophets is simply to add a new ethical horror to the dismal delusion of life, and to fall back into the pessimism of Omar Khayyám.

Baptized fatalism.

" We are no other than a moving row
    Of Magic Shadow-shapes, that come and go
    Round with this Sun-illumined Lantern, held
    In Midnight by the Master of the Show;

" Impotent Pieces of the Game He plays
    Upon this Checker-board of Nights and Days;
    Hither and thither moves, and checks, and slays,
    And one by one back in the Closet lays.

" The Moving Finger writes; and, having writ,
    Moves on; nor all your Piety nor wit
    Shall lure it back to cancel half a Line,
    Nor all your tears wash out a Word of it.

" And that inverted Bowl they call the Sky,
    Whereunder crawling coop'd we live and die,
    Lift not your hands to It for help—for it
    As impotently rolls as you or I." [1]

[1] *Rubáiyát of Omar Khayyám*. Rendered into English verse by Edward Fitzgerald, with an accompaniment of drawings by Elihu Vedder (Boston, 1884), stanzas 72, 73, 75, 76.

II

*Is determin-
ism proved?*

This is the solution which modern positivism, christened or unchristened, offers for the problem of the freedom of the will. Before we turn to consider the very different answer which Christ gives to the same question, let us stay for a moment to ask whether this current and popular solution is of the nature of a demonstration, or of the nature of a doubt. Is it so clearly proven that science forces us to accept determinism? Or is it an unverifiable assumption, which is made under the influence of a general scepticism in regard to spiritual realities, and which leaves out of view quite as many and quite as important facts as those which it professes to explain? Are we compelled to admit it; or is it only one of two alternatives, neither of which is scientifically demonstrable, so that the choice between them must rest upon other considerations?

I do not hesitate to say that the whole weight of sober and sane criticism inclines to the latter conclusion. Determinism has not yet been established either by physiological, psychological, or metaphysical argument.

*Philosophy
says no.*

The common assumption that the abstract reasoning of Jonathan Edwards against the liberty of the will has never been and cannot be refuted, is based upon ignorance of the facts. An American philosopher, Mr. Rowland Hazard, has answered it with great clearness and force. Professor George P. Fisher says : " The fundamental point of Mr. Hazard's criticism of Edwards is fully established. It must be allowed that his confutation of that conception of the will which underlies the reasoning of the great theologian is sound and conclusive." [1]

Science says no.

The support which modern science is supposed to give to the theory of determinism turns out, upon closer examination, to be altogether illusory. The soundest and most careful investigators utterly decline to commit themselves to that metaphysical dogma, or to bind out science as a maid-of-all-work in the service of fatalistic theology.

Free-will a daily miracle.

The most distinguished of living English scientists recently said : " The influence of animal or vegetable life on matter is infinitely beyond the range of any scientific inquiry hitherto entered on. Its power of directing the motions of moving particles, *in the demonstrated daily miracle of our human free-will*, and

[1] Rowland Hazard, *Freedom of Mind in Willing* (Boston, Houghton, Mifflin & Co., 1889). Introduction by George P. Fisher, p. xxxi.

in the growth of generation after generation of plants from a single seed, are infinitely different from any possible result of the fortuitous concourse of atoms. The real phenomena of life infinitely transcend human science."[1] The theory that consciousness is a function of the brain breaks down completely when it attempts to explain the phenomena of sleep. Why should all the other functions of the body be carried on without fatigue and without interruption while this alone demands rest and admits of intervals of cessation? If consciousness is a function of nerve-matter, sleep abolishes it. How does it come back again without losing the sense of personal identity?

Thought is not a secretion.

Is it conceivable that the highest character, the loftiest genius, is purely an intermittent secretion of certain nerve-cells, and that during the hours of sleep, embracing one-third of its entire history, it is absolutely non-existent? "Function," says an eminent neurologist, "is a physiological term, and it is, I submit, improper to speak of states of consciousness as being functions of the brain. . . . It is not the mind, but the physical basis of mind, which is a product of physical evolution. It is the

[1] Lord Kelvin (Sir William Thomson), in *The Fortnightly Review*, March, 1892.

organ of mind, not the mind of itself, which being an evolution out of the rest of the body is representative of it." [1]

The fact that the brain is a double organ, — that there are really two brains, only one of which is used, — cannot be explained on the theory that consciousness is merely the result of the vibration of nerve filaments, as the music of the Æolian harp is the result of the passage of the wind over its strings. A distinguished physiologist has cleverly shown that if this were the case a double brain would mean a double amount of thought, just as twice the number of strings would mean twice the quantity of music.[2] But the fact that this is not so, points clearly to the hypothesis that the brain is not an Æolian harp helplessly vibrating under external impulses, but a double organ with two sets of keys, and the mind is like the player who can use either one of them to make the music. And this corresponds closely with our own sense of the process. For we are conscious not only of passive thoughts and

The brain the organ of the mind.

---

[1] Dr. J. Hughlings Jackson, "Lecture on the Comparative Study of Diseases of the Nervous System" (*British Medical Journal*, August 17, 1889).

[2] Dr. William H. Thomson, *Materialism and Modern Physiology of the Nervous System* (New York, Putnams, 1892), pp. 83 ff.

feelings, evoked within us by external causes, but also of thoughts and feelings voluntarily directed and combined, woven together in creative harmonies, and moving under the guidance of chosen ideals towards a symphonic completeness. Even the sense of discord and conflict which often rises within us is an evidence that there is a player as well as an instrument. For it is inconceivable that an Æolian harp, ill-strung, should dislike its own bad music, and endeavour, or think that it could endeavour, to make a better, sweeter sound.

Heredity not final. Heredity is undoubtedly a real and powerful force. It supplies the outfit of life. But does it determine the use which we shall make of it? The very extension of the doctrine by the investigations of science dissolves this narrow and absolute conclusion. We inherit from thousands, from hundreds of thousands, of ancestors. The blood of many families and tribes and races is mingled in our veins. What is it that decides which of these many lines we shall follow? It must be either blind chance or free choice. All the phenomena of society, all the facts of consciousness, are in favour of the latter supposition. We see men whose heritage is of the lowest and the worst, working their way up, by sheer strength of moral choice and effort, to a higher plane. We see men whose heritage is of the loftiest and the best, declining

> "thro' acted crime,
> Or seeming-genial venial fault,
> Recurring and suggesting still,"[1]

to the very depths of infamy. It is true that a man cannot bring out of himself anything that is not already there. But it is true also, by virtue of heredity, that there are many potential men in every man, and which of them is to emerge, he chooses for himself by a thousand silent moral preferences ; by yielding or by resisting; by the cowardice and corruption, or by the courage and purification of his own free-will.

Even those who write of human life from a professedly naturalistic standpoint cannot get rid of this conviction. Take Zola, for example. If he were consistent, he would speak with equal and impassive coldness of all his characters, tangled together in the inextricable toils of heredity. But he cannot help letting his hatred and contempt for the selfish, the luxurious, the vicious, express itself in the very accent with which he describes them. He cannot help showing his admiration and affec-

Moral judgments assume liberty.

[1] Tennyson's poem, *Will.*

tion for those who, like *Denise* and *Doctor Pascal*, and *Clotilde*, rise out of the infamy which envelops the family *Rougon-Macquart*. Virtue and vice may be scientifically treated as if they were merely natural products like sugar and vitriol ; but when we come to talk of them from a human and humane standpoint, there is something within us which demands that we shall recognize a merit in being virtuous, and a shame in being vicious, — qualities which can never belong to mere secretions, whether of plants or of nerves, — qualities which have no possible meaning unless there is a free-will in man, capable of choosing between the evil and the good.

The testimony of modern psychology. Now that a free-will is possible, modern psychology assures us, as the result of its latest researches. It does not attempt to demonstrate the existence of such a power by physiological investigation. It confesses that this demonstration is impossible with our present knowledge. But it declares with equal candour that the contrary attempt to show that the sense of freedom is a delusion, is inconclusive. " The last word of psychology here," says Professor William James, " is ignorance, for the forces engaged are too delicate and numerous to be followed in detail." He points out the ex-

tremely reckless and inconsequent nature of
the reasoning by which the determinists seek
to make mere analogies drawn from the course
of rivers, and reflex actions, and other material
phenomena, serve as proofs that the will is a
mechanical effect. He exposes the bold assumption by which they ignore the testimony
of consciousness in the presence of feeling and
effort. He shows that the utmost which any
argument for determinism can do is to present
a possible hypothesis, which a man who has
already determined to hold fast to the idea
that the whole universe is one chain of inevitable causation may accept if he likes. But
meanwhile the other alternative stands equally
open. The moral arguments all point in that
direction. The only course, in such a situa- *Free-will is*
tion, is voluntary choice. "For scepticism it- *possible.*
self, if systematic, is also voluntary choice. If,
meanwhile, the will be indetermined, it would
seem only fitting that the belief in its inde-
termination should be voluntarily chosen from
amongst other possible beliefs. Freedom's
first deed should be to affirm itself. . . .
Thus not only our morality but our religion,
so far as the latter is deliberate, depends on
the effort which we can make. '*Will you or
won't you have it so ?*' is the most probing

Q

question we are ever asked : we are asked it
every hour of the day, and about the largest
as well as the smallest, the most theoretical as
well as the most practical, things. We answer
by consents or non-consents, and not by words.
What wonder if these dumb responses should
seem our deepest organs of communication
with the nature of things ! What wonder if
the effort demanded by them should be the
measure of our worth as men ! What wonder
if the amount which we accord of it be the
one strictly underived and original contribu-
tion which we make to the world ! " [1]

III

Christ says liberty is real.

Here, then, modern science, careful, exact
reverent, as distinguished from modern scepticism, leaves us before the two doors. And
here Christ comes to us, calling us to enter
through the door of liberty into the pathway of
eternal life. " Ask, and it shall be given you;
seek and ye shall find; knock and it shall be
opened unto you." [2] "If any man willeth to
do His will, he shall know of the teaching." [3]

[1] William James, *Psychology*, vol. ii., p. 579.
[2] St. Matt. vii. 7.
[3] St. John vii. 17.

The whole life and ministry of Jesus is a *The life of* revelation of moral freedom. His entrance *Jesus, a* *revelation of* into the world was voluntary. His continu- *free-will.* ance in human life was voluntary. His death was voluntary. At the first crisis of His life He chose to go about His Father's business. In the temptation He chose to resist the allure- ments of the Evil One. On the way to the cross He chose not to call on God for the deliverance which He knew would come in answer to His call. He was, indeed, fulfilling an appointed task, treading the path which had been marked out for the feet of the Christ; but He was fulfilling the task freely; He was walking in liberty because He loved to do the will of God. The triumph of His virtue lay in the freedom of His choice.

There was a singular propriety in the text of *The preach-* His first public discourse. It was a declaration *ing of Jesus,* *a gospel of* of liberty, as well as of grace. It was an eman- *liberty.* cipation proclamation as well as a gospel of com- fort and help. " The spirit of the Lord is upon me, because He anointed me to preach good tidings to the poor; He hath sent me to pro- claim release to the captives, and recovering of sight to the blind, to set at liberty them that are crushed, to proclaim the acceptable year of the Lord."[1] And what was the oppressive bondage from which He proclaimed release? Was it not the tyranny of a false doctrine of necessity over the minds of men, as well as the enslaving influence of sin over their inert and hopeless wills?

*The Phari-
sees taught
Fate.*
Here were the scribes and Pharisees teaching that the whole world was divided into two classes, — the chosen and the not-chosen, the righteous for whom salvation was secure whatever they might do, and the sinners for whom salvation was impossible whatever they might do. Here were the outcast, the lost, the neglected, shut out, by no choice of their own, but by their birth, by the occupations in which they were engaged, by their ignorance, by the very conditions of their life, from all part in the kingdom of heaven as the scribes and Pharisees conceived it; not only the harlots and the publicans, but also *Am Haarez*, "the people of the land," with whom it was not fitting that a righteous person should have any dealings;[2] miserable souls, bound by inheritance to a desperate and unhallowed fate. Here came Jesus, taking His way directly to these lost ones, these outsiders, and telling them that all this doctrine of inevitable doom was a chain

[1] St. Luke iv. 18.   [2] Bruce, *Kingdom of God*, 145.

of lies, breaking the imaginary fetters from their souls and assuring them by His first word that they were free, even though they were ignorant of it. "Repent," He cried, "for the kingdom of heaven has approached unto you."[1] "Except ye be converted and become as little children, ye shall not enter into the kingdom of heaven."[2] And what is the significance of these words, "repentance" and "conversion,"—their real significance, I mean, not that which has been read into them by centuries of false and formal theology? They are not passive and involuntary words; they do not rest upon the idea of qualifications which may or may not be in the possession of those to whom Christ speaks. They are active words, — words of inward movement and exertion. "Repent" means change your mind; make that simple effort of the soul for internal change which is the ultimate act of the free will;[3] put forth

Jesus taught Freedom.

[1] St. Matt. iv. 17.

[2] St. Matt. xviii. 3.

[3] "Every intelligent being, capable of conceiving of higher ethical conditions than he has yet attained, has in his own moral nature for the exercise of his creative powers an infinite sphere, within which . . . he is the supreme disposer. . . . A man who does not want to be pure and noble, may yet begin one step lower in the scale of moral advancement, with the wish to want to be pure and noble ; and, here commencing the cultivation of his moral nature, ascend from this lower

that power of fixed attention to the new motive
which is the central essence of liberty and the
creative force of the soul.[1] "Be converted,"
as Christ spoke the word, is not passive; it
expresses an action exercised by the soul within
itself; it means simply "turn around"; set
yourself in a new relation to God, to truth, to
virtue. The name of this relation is faith.
"Believe" is Christ's great word. It is the
"*open sesame*" of the kingdom. "Believe in
God, believe also in Me."[2] "He that believeth
hath everlasting life."[3] "All things are possible
to him that believeth."[4] But it is never spoken
of as a mere intellectual opinion, or emotional
experience, an irresistible conviction wrought
by external evidence in the mind, or bestowed
without effort upon the soul. The Bible never
says that faith is a gift. There is a voluntary
element in it. It is something to be done by
the exercise of an inward power. It is a coming of the soul to Christ; it is a following of the

Faith is free.

point, through the want to be pure and noble, to the free effort
to gratify this want." — ROWLAND HAZARD, *Freedom of
Mind in Willing*, "Of Effort for Internal Change" (Boston, Houghton, Mifflin & Co., 1889), chap. xiv.

[1] "The essential achievement of the will when it is most
'voluntary,' is to *attend* to a difficult object and hold it fast
before the mind." — JAMES, *Psychology*, vol. ii., p. 561.

[2] St. John xiv. 1.   [3] St. John vi. 47.   [4] St. Mark ix. 23.

soul after Him; it is the first step in a long course of spiritual activity. It is a deed. The disciples said unto Christ, "What must we do that we may work the works of God?" Jesus answered, "This is the work of God, that ye believe on Him whom He hath sent."[1]

Now there is not a hint in all the teaching of Jesus that this first act of freedom is impossible for any soul to whom He speaks. He has no idea of an eternal predestination binding some to belief and others to unbelief, a secret decree including certain men in the kingdom and excluding others from all possibility of entering into it. It is true that He says, "No man can come unto Me except the Father draw him";[2] but what He means by this drawing He tells us in the parable of the Lost Son, where it is the simple knowledge of the Father's abundant love that draws the prodigal back from the far country of sin;[3] and in the parable of the Publican in the Temple,[4] where it is the sense of the Divine mercy and forgiveness that makes the outcast man cry, "God, be merciful to me a sinner." There is prevenient grace in the doctrine of Jesus. But the grace is there. It has already come. All that man has to do is to meet it, to

All may believe.

---

[1] St. John vi. 28, 29. [3] St. Luke xv.
[2] St. John vi. 44. [4] St. Luke xviii. 10–14.

put himself into the upward swing of it, that it may lift and help him heavenward.

Christ is God's call to faith.

A calling and a choosing by God are necessary before any man can be saved. But Jesus does not speak of this choosing and calling as eternal. Christ Himself is the call, and all who answer it are chosen. "If any man thirst, let him come unto Me and drink."[1] "Him that cometh unto Me I will in no wise cast out."[2] The heavenly invitation is set forth in all its generosity and sincerity in the story of the Marriage Feast.[3] The bidding went out into the highways and hedges, to the bad and to the good; and all who heard and accepted it were welcome. And if a single guest was turned away, it was only because his own conduct showed that he had not really taken the invitation honestly and accepted willingly all that was provided for him.

No predestination to death.

There is not a single word in all that Jesus said to suggest any other reason than this for the exclusion of a single person from the blessings of the kingdom. "*Ye will not* come unto Me that ye might have life."[4] "How often would I have gathered thy children together even as a hen gathereth her chickens under

[1] St. John vii. 37. [3] St. Matt. xxii. 1–14.
[2] St. John vi. 37. [4] St. John v. 40.

her wings, *and ye would not.*"[1] There is not
one statement that anything else but mercy
and grace has been eternally prepared by God
for any human soul. In that awful parable of
judgment which discloses the convincing picture
of the final separation of the evil from the
good, Christ says distinctly that the joy of
the blessed has been prepared for them from
the foundation of the world, but of the punishment of the cursed, He says with equal dis-
tinctness that it was not prepared for them,
but for the devil and his angels.[2] No one is
ever lost because he cannot do good, but only
because he will not do what he can.

Christ recognizes the undoubted truth which
lies in the doctrine of heredity; but He exposes, and almost ridicules, the false and
fatal extremes to which men think it out.
To the Jews, who claimed that because they
were Abraham's seed they must be free, He
showed that they were in bondage to their
own sins. They had chosen to break away
from the heredity of faith and righteousness,
and were no longer the true children of Abraham. They had become the children of the
devil, because they had "willed to do his
works."[3] He said to His disciples who took

Christ on heredity.

---

[1] St. Matt. xxiii. 37.   [2] St. Matt. xxv. 34–41.
[3] St. John viii. 33–47.

up the cant of the day about hereditary sin and
punishment, asked whether the blind man or
his parents had sinned that he was born blind,
"Neither hath this man sinned, nor his parents,
but that the works of God should be made
manifest in him."[1] The true inheritance, the
deepest inheritance which Jesus recognizes in
the human race, is an inheritance from God;
a nature made in the Divine image, spiritual,
free, responsible, and capable, though so sadly
marred, though so far astray, of returning to
communion with the Heavenly Father.

The weak-ness of man. Undoubtedly Christ perceived and taught
the immense difficulty of being good; the in-
firmity which long centuries of sin has wrought
into the very fibres of the soul; the awful
and almost inaccessible height of true holiness; the enormous obstacles which lie in the
way of attaining it. The gate is strait, and
we must agonize to enter in by it. The
road is steep, and we must toil to climb it.
"How hardly shall they that have riches enter
into the kingdom of God."[2] And yet "the
kingdom of heaven suffereth violence, and men
of violence take it by force."[3] There is an
effort which succeeds even in this greatest
of all endeavours, not in its own strength,

---

[1] St. John ix. 3.   [2] St. Mark x. 23.
[3] St. Matt. xi. 12.

but because it is sure of a Divine assistance. *The grace of God.*
"With man it is impossible, but not with
God."[1] To the human will, enfeebled and
corrupted, so that it is like a sick man, barely
able to turn himself upon his couch, and look
and long and cry for help, three great sources
of strength are always open and accessible.

The first is prayer. "Men ought always to *Prayer.*
pray, and not to faint."[2] How sweet and
serene is the voice that rings through the vain
disputations and doubtful wranglings of the
scribes and Pharisees, and calls every sinful
soul to pray! Pray! you may not be able to
realize your own ideal, but you can ask God
to help you hold fast to it and struggle towards
it. Pray!

> "More things are wrought by prayer
> Than this world dreams of."[3]

Pray! For God is not deaf, nor sleeping, nor
gone upon a journey; He has not bound you
to an inexorable fate and bound Himself not to
interfere with it. Pray! The liberty of your
own soul, and the liberty of God Himself, dwells
in that word; for when you stretch your feeble
hand to Him, a Divine hand will meet it, and

---

[1] St. Mark x. 27.   [2] St. Luke xviii. 1.
[3] Tennyson, *The Passing of Arthur.*

break your fetters, and lift you out of darkness and death into life and light.

The Holy Spirit. The second source of strength is the Holy Spirit. It is inconceivable, morally impossible, that there should be such a Spirit, and yet that His influence should be withheld from those who need and implore it. "If ye then, being evil, know how to give good gifts unto your children, how much more shall your heavenly Father give the Holy Spirit unto them that ask Him." [1]

Christ our Helper. The third source of strength is Christ Himself. Does the sense of past guilt stand in the way of future effort? He says, "I have power on earth to forgive sins." [2] Does the soul feel dead and hopeless under the burden of evil habits? He says, "I came that they may have life, and may have it abundantly." [3] Do the works of a true and vital righteousness seem far beyond our power? He says, "Without Me ye can do nothing;" [4] but, "Lo, I am with you alway, even unto the end of the world." [5] "He that believeth on Me, the works that I do shall he do also, and greater works than these shall he do, because I go unto the Father." [6] The whole

---

[1] St. Luke xi. 13.
[2] St. Mark ii. 10.
[3] St. John x. 10.
[4] St. John xv. 5.
[5] St. Matt. xxviii. 20.
[6] St. John xiv. 12.

life of Christ is summed up in the words, "But as many as received Him, to them *gave He power to become the sons of God.*" [1]

But this receiving, we need to remember and assert again and again, is not a passive thing. It is an action of the soul, the opening of a door within the heart, the welcoming of a heavenly master. God does not save men as a watchmaker who repairs and sets a watch, but as a King who recalls his servants to their duty, as a Father who makes new revelations of His love to draw His lost children back to Himself. The dogmas of the schools in regard to the working out of what they call the scheme of redemption sound like the creak and rattle of some vast machine. The doctrine of Christ is like the soft breath of spring, evoking the songs of birds and the unfolding of new life. No fiery chariot of grace swoops down to snatch men to glory. But a living Messenger comes forth from God to ask men to turn and walk back with Him to their soul's home. The invitation itself is a guarantee of the power to accept it. With authority Christ commanded the winds and the sea and they obeyed Him. But with gracious pleading He invited the hearts of men, and those that were willing gladly heard and followed Him.

The way of deliverance.

[1] St. John i. 12.

God helps those who help themselves.

"If any man *wills* to come after Me," [1]—that is the prelude of His message. He offers a leadership to men who can follow, a mastership to men who can obey. Out of this first movement He promises to guide and direct the whole development of the new life, — not a passive life of retirement, of ascetic meditation, of reflection upon secret truth, — but an active life of service, of warfare against evil in the world, a life which translates truth into conduct.

Christus Liberator.

Contrast the religion of Jesus in this respect with the Oriental religions, and with those forms of Christianity which have borrowed the garments of Buddha and speak with the accent of Mahomet. They despise and slight personality. Christ respects and emphasizes it. They aim to reduce and evaporate responsibility. Christ aims to deepen and increase it. They point forward to a blank Nirvana in which the individual is lost and absorbed, or a Paradise in which he is forever lapped in sensual ease and pleasure. Christ speaks of the perfecting of the individual through the Divine communion and service on earth, and his entrance in heaven upon a new stage of the same communion, the same service, — "not in a blessed idleness, but in an exalted

[1] St. Matt. xvi. 24.

kingly work and activity." And the entrance
to this kingdom on earth, the continuance in
its realm of liberty, the attainment of its final
glory, are all through an act of the will. The
freedom which originated in God is only to be
preserved by returning to God and abiding in
Him.

> "Our wills are ours, we know not how;
> Our wills are ours, to make them Thine."[1]

That is the teaching of Jesus. That is the
truth which, when it comes to men, makes
them and keeps them free.

IV

It is impossible that we should be faithful
preachers of Christ to the present age, unless
we preach this truth. There may have been
ages in which it was important to dwell upon
other sides and aspects of the manifold reality
of the spiritual world. But to-day this is the
important side; this is the aspect which demands a clear recognition and an unfaltering
proclamation by those who mean to be true to
Christ and loyal to the needs of humanity. I
do not believe that there is a single passage in
the Old Testament which contradicts Christ's

The age needs this message.

[1] Tennyson, *In Memoriam*, Proem.

doctrine of the real liberty of the soul. But
if there were such a passage, I would leave it
forever alone, as belonging to that knowledge
which was in part, and which was done away
when that which was perfect had come. I do
not believe that there is a single word in the
St. Paul on writings of St. Paul which stands against this
freedom. doctrine of the real liberty of the soul. I
cut loose from the false interpretations which
men have read into his words. I take the
light of Christ's teaching in my hand, and I
go back to interpret by that light the teachings of the great Epistle to the Romans with
its glorious revelation of " the mystery which
hath been kept in silence through times eternal, but now is manifested, and by the Scriptures
of the prophets, according to the commandment
of the eternal God, is made known unto all
the nations *unto obedience of faith.*" [1] I hear
again the cry of the struggling, labouring, conquering apostle : " *To will is present with me,
but to do that which is good is not. . . .* O
wretched man that I am, who shall deliver me
out of the body of this death ? I thank God
through Christ Jesus our Lord ;" [2] and I know
that St. Paul also was a believer in the freedom of the will, and that he received this

[1] Rom. xvi. 26.   [2] Rom. vii. 18, 24, 25.

gospel and the power to fulfil it, through the proclamation of liberty in Jesus Christ.

"This matter of free-will," wrote one of the most orthodox of theologians, but a few years before his death, "underlies everything. If you bring it to question, it is infinitely more than Calvinism. . . . I believe in Calvinism, and I say that free-will stands before Calvinism. Everything is gone if free-will is gone ; the moral system is gone, if free-will is gone ; you cannot escape except by Materialism on the one hand or by Pantheism on the other. Hold hard therefore to the doctrine of free-will."[1]

Free-will the pressing question.

Yes, and we may say more than this. Not only is the moral system gone, but the great attraction of Christ is gone, the power of His gospel to liberate men is gone, if free-will is gone.

The age has hypnotized itself. It is drifting steadily towards fatalism. It denies freedom, and therefore it is not free. It is in bondage to its own doubt. It is enslaved by its own denial. If there is such a thing as liberty, it can only be developed, as everything else has been developed, by action, by exercise.

The age has hypnotized itself.

[1] A. A. Hodge, *Popular Lectures on Theological Themes* (Philadelphia, 1887), p. 184.

R

Life is self-change to meet environment. Liberty is self-exertion to unfold the soul. The law of natural selection is that those who use a faculty shall expand it, but those who use it not shall lose it. Religion is life, and it must grow under the laws of life. Faith is simply the assertion of spiritual freedom ; it is the first adventure of the soul. Make that adventure towards God, make that adventure towards Christ, and the soul will know that it is alive. So it enters upon that upward course which leads through the liberty of the sons of God to the height of heaven,

> " Where love is an unerring light
> And joy its own security." [1]

We must proclaim liberty in Christ.

This is the truth with which we are to go out a-gospelling in this age of doubt. We are to tell men that though much has been determined for them by causes beyond their control, — their circumstances, their talents, their faculties, — one thing has not been determined, and that is what they will do with them. Much has been ordained before their birth, — their nationality, their family, their station in life, — but one thing has not been ordained, and that is whether they are to move from this starting-

[1] Wordsworth, *Ode to Duty.*

point towards life or towards death. They may be like men sunken in a nightmare dream of helplessness, muttering in their sleep, " If I am to be saved, I shall be saved ; if I am to be lost, I shall be lost," — but we must cry to them with the voice of the Spirit : " Awake, thou that sleepest, and arise from the dead, and Christ shall give thee light."

VII

SOVEREIGNTY

"I say to thee, do thou repeat
   To the first man thou mayest meet
   In lane, highway, or open street —

"That he and we and all men move
   Under a canopy of love,
   As broad as the blue sky above;

"That doubt and trouble, fear and pain
   And anguish, all are shadows vain,
   That death itself shall not remain;

"That weary deserts we may tread,
   A dreary labyrinth may thread,
   Through dark ways underground be led;

"Yet if we will one Guide obey,
   The dreariest path, the darkest way,
   Shall issue out in heavenly day;

"And we, on divers shores now cast,
   Shall meet, our perilous voyage past,
   All in our Father's house at last."

—RICHARD CHENEVIX TRENCH,
   The Kingdom of God.

VII

SOVEREIGNTY

THE questions about the world which science considers and answers, all have to do with secondary causes. Beyond that sphere she does not need to go, and within that sphere her wisdom is sufficient. We come to her like curious children. We "want to see the wheels go round." We want to know what the wheels are made of. She tells us, and there she stops. All that we have a right to ask of her is that she shall be true to facts, and that she shall confine herself to them. When the astronomer Laplace was reproached for not mentioning God in his treatise on the dynamics of the solar system, he answered, "I had no need of that hypothesis." And this reply was just, as Mr. John Fiske has pointed out, because "in order to give a specific explanation of any single group of phenomena, it would not do to appeal to divine action, which is equally the source of all phenomena." [1]

[1] *Christian Literature*, January, 1896, "The Everlasting Reality of Religion," p. 306.

The great questions lie beyond them.

But the moment we take this reasonable and modest position (and it is a great pity that theology has not been more ready to take it), we perceive that curiosity in regard to single groups of phenomena by no means satisfies or exhausts the activity of the questioning spirit in man. There is a deeper curiosity in regard to the relation of these single groups of phenomena to each other, and to ourselves, and to the possibility of a meaning, a purpose, an end, underlying all things and all their workings. Out of this deeper curiosity rise the questions which are most urgent and vital, — questions which, when we consider them abstractly, are philosophical, and condition the unity of our intellectual life; but when we consider them personally, they are religious, and upon their answer our spiritual peace and moral action absolutely depend. How are we to think about the things that we know? What are we to believe in regard to the things that science tells us we cannot know, but which we still feel are necessary conditions of all intelligent and right conduct? Is there an invisible unity beneath all the visible diversity of phenomena? What is the nature of that unity, personal or impersonal, conscious or unconscious? Is there anything behind the mechanical working of the world, now so wonderfully explained, which corresponds to what there is in us when we make and use a machine or an instrument, when we plant and cultivate a garden, or when we select and train a noble race of animals? Is there a final cause towards which things work together, and a supreme power which guides them to that end?

This is the question of sovereignty. We can no more help asking it than we can help thinking. *The question of sovereignty.*

We are in the world like voyagers on a ship. We inquire what the ship is made of; and science tells us, — iron and wood. And what makes it float? The buoyancy of the air which it contains. And what makes it go? Steam. And what makes the steam? The heat of the furnace. Then, if we are sufficiently interested, science takes us down into the engine-room, and shows us all the condensers and pistons and cranks and wheels, more fully than they have ever been shown before; and we are amazed and profoundly grateful. We come up again into the light of day. We look into the overarching heaven, the home of sunshine and storm, the deep mother of light and darkness. We look out upon the great and wide sea, full of mystery and terror. New questionings spring to our lips. Where is the ship going? Is there a captain on board? Does he know, does he care, what is to become of it? Is he wise, is he faithful, is he a good captain? Can he direct the vessel through tempests and dangers? Can he tell us how to work with him, how to act in times of peril and perplexity? Can we be sure of him, can we trust him?

Now to this questioning, scepticism gives a reply of desperate uncertainty; and positivism answers with a stern and sullen, No! The world is a derelict vessel, and we are masterless and lost mariners. This answer has been expressed by a French poet in powerful and pathetic verse.

> " Jouet de l'ouragan, qui l'emporte et le mène,
>   Encombré de tresors et d'agrès submergés,
> Ce navire perdu, mais c'est le nef humaine,
>   Et nous sommes les naufragés.
>
> " L'equipage affolé manœuvre en vain dans l'ombre;
>   L'Épouvante est à bord, le Désespoir, le Deuil;
> Assise au gouvernail, la Fatalité sombre
>   Le dirige vers un écueil." [1]

But Christ gives a very different answer. It seems as if His very words were chosen to contradict this view of life as a helpless, hope-

---

[1] L. Ackerman, *Ma Vie, Poesies*, etc. (Paris, 1885), " Le Cri," p. 180.

less voyage, and humanity as a shipwrecked *Christ answers, Yes.* race. For what is it that He says to His disciples as they look out upon the mystery of existence?

"Seek not what ye shall eat, and what ye shall drink, *neither be ye as a ship that is tossed on the waves of a tempestuous sea* (μὴ μετεωρί-ζεσθε), for your Father knoweth that ye have need of these things." [1]

The vessel is not driving masterless over the ocean. The Captain is on board. He is God. He is also our Father. For all who trust and serve Him, it is a sure voyage, a certain port, a safe harbour.

I

The doctrine of the presence and sovereignty *The sovereignty of God.* of God in His world, in one form or another, is essential to the validity of any reasoning which attempts to go beyond the mere appearance of things. Without it we find ourselves, as one has well said, "put to permanent intellectual confusion." Without it the world lies before us, as Pope wrote in the first draft of his *Essay on Man*, —

"A mighty maze, and all without a plan."

[1] St. Luke xii. 29.

And if we follow the poet in that cold philosophical deism which led him to revise his famous line so that it now reads

"A mighty maze, but not without a plan,"[1]

we are still in the dark, still confused and hopeless, unless we go further and learn enough of Him who made the plan, to trust Him even when we cannot perfectly understand His working, and to confide absolutely in "His most holy, wise, and powerful preserving and governing all His creatures and all their actions."[2]

Christ's view of it.

This is what Christ gives us : a view of God in His world which requires faith to accept it, but which when it is accepted, satisfies the reason and the heart better than any other view, clears away many of the intellectual and moral difficulties which beset us, and becomes the inward source not of doubt and distress, but of certainty and peace.

Contrasted with other views.

This is not true, we must admit, of some of the forms in which the doctrine of divine sovereignty has been preached in Christ's name. They have often disregarded the facts of nature. They have often outraged the moral instincts of humanity. They have created new obstacles to faith. They have driven men

[1] Pope's *Essay on Man*, part i., line 6.
[2] *The Shorter Catechism*, question xi.

back in dumb resentment to believe in the positivist's "sombre Fatality," rather than in an absentee God who has foreordained, by one and the same decree, all the evil and all the good, all the sorrow and shame and suffering that are in the world.

Not so with Christ's teaching. It is sane and sweet. It allays resentment and begets serenity. It gives a reconciling, harmonizing, atoning view of God's sovereignty. And if we can see it clearly and preach it faithfully, it will be to-day, as it was in His day, one of the great attractions of the gospel for an age of doubt.

II

Christ's doctrine of the divine sovereignty was both old and new. It was old because it recognized the truth, uttered so magnificently by prophets and psalmists, of God's right and power to rule the universe which He has made. "Thy throne, O God, is for ever and ever."[1] "The Lord hath prepared His throne in the heavens and His kingdom ruleth over all."[2] "He doeth according to His will in the army of heaven, and among the inhabitants of the earth: and none can stay His hand, or say unto Him, What doest Thou?"[3]

Christ's doctrine old and new.

[1] Psalm xlv. 6. [2] Psalm ciii. 19. [3] Daniel iv. 35.

A simpler revelation.

But Christ's doctrine was new because it revealed the presence of the sovereign God in the physical universe more simply, more naturally, more intimately, than it had ever been revealed before. How gentle, how plain, how mildly luminous, is the language in which Jesus expresses this truth, compared with the flashing, rolling speech of the prophets! He uses the words of common life, transfigured with emotion, — the language of lyric, rather than of epic, poetry.

God in His world.

The manifestations of divine power in the Old Testament appear chiefly as mighty works, exceptional forthputtings of supernal force. It seems sometimes as if they came from a distance ; as if God had withdrawn from the world and had been called back to it by the peril and the cry of His people. But Christ would teach us to feel that He has never gone away for an instant. He is always here. Nothing that happens is hidden from Him. Nor does He hide Himself from any who would behold Him. We may see Him every day, in the feeding of the birds, in the blossoming of the flowers,

" And every wayside bush aflame with God."

In all the processes of nature He is present and sovereign.

This view of the relation of God to the material world is not external and mechanical. It is inward and vital. God has not made the world and wound it up and left it to run by itself. He is in it, as really as a man is in the house that he inhabits, and all the potencies that move and animate it flow directly from Him. The Jews thought that God had fabricated the universe in six days and sat down to rest on the seventh, laying aside His work as a clock-maker would put down a finished clock. But Christ said, "My Father worketh until now, and I work."[1] Creation is not ended, it is going on all the time. Yesterday was a creative day; and so is to-day; and so to-morrow will be. The divine thought is still weaving its beautiful garment on the roaring loom of Time.

The divine immanence.

But God's activity in the world is not capricious or disorderly. No one was more sensitive than Jesus to "the rhythmic element in nature, — the flow of rivers, the procession of stars, the antiphony of day and night, the silent but inviolate order of the seasons."[2] It was He who expressed the law of growth :

The divine orderliness.

[1] St. John v. 17.
[2] H. W. Mabie, *Essays on Nature and Culture* (New York, 1896), p. 295.

"first the blade, then the ear, and after that the full corn in the ear."[1] It was He who suggested the analogy of natural law in the spiritual world, applying the figure of germination to His own death and resurrection: "Except a corn of wheat fall into the ground and die, it abideth alone; but if it die, it bringeth forth much fruit."[2] The parables which He used to describe the kingdom of heaven were drawn from nature and based on law. It was like "leaven which a woman took and hid in three measures of meal until the whole was leavened," or "like a grain of mustard seed, which a man took and sowed in his field; which indeed is the least of all seeds, but when it is grown it is the greatest among herbs."[3] He taught His disciples to look upon the regular and steadfast ordinances of nature as the proof that their Heavenly Father was mindful of them and would take care of them. You will not find any such superfluous phrase as "special Providence" in the teaching of Jesus. His thought was of a general and universal Providence, wide enough and deep enough to embrace the wants of all creatures and provide for them. God's chil-

[1] St. Mark iv. 28.   [2] St. John xii. 24.
[3] St. Matt. xiii. 32, 33.

dren were not to trust in miracles and marvels
for their daily bread ; they were not to be
always looking and calling for the extraordinary, — manna from the sky, water from the
riven rock. They were to rest rather upon
the course of nature in quiet confidence, and
work with it in cheerful joy, knowing that
He who clothes the grass of the field will much
more clothe them,[1] — and by the same power
working in the same way.

Yet Jesus did not think of God as having *Miracles not*
exhausted all possible modes of His activity *against*
in those which are familiar to us. His pres- *nature.*
ence in the world is of such a personal kind
that it necessarily brings with it the power of
direct, personal, infinitely varied action. Out
of this power spring those strange signs and
wondrous works which we call miracles. Jesus
never said that they were against nature. He
never even said that they were supernatural.
He claimed only that they were proofs of a
divine mission, because they were such works
as could only come from God. They were
signs, just as all uncommon and extraordinary *Signs of*
acts are signs. But signs of what? Of per- *personality.*
sonality, of that power of choice in modes of

[1] St. Matt. vi. 30.

s

action which is the essential attribute of a free spirit. They were wrought in order that men might believe, not in order that they might be astonished; and just as truly in order that they might believe in the order of nature as in the Person who upholds it by His presence.

The reign of God through law.

"An energy," says Mr. Ruskin, "may be natural without being normal, and divine without being constant." Jesus did not teach the reign of law. He taught the reign of God through law. And in order that men might be sure that the law did not bind God like a chain, but freely expressed His sovereign will, it was given unto Jesus to show men those rare works, unique and transcendent, like strokes of genius, which reveal, as if by flashes of light, the true relation between the sovereign God and the universe which He is making and ruling.

The secret of Jesus.

It is always to this personal God that Jesus would direct the thoughts and confident affections of men. How is it possible for any one to miss His meaning, and translate it into something entirely different, as Matthew Arnold does in his misinterpretation of what he calls "the secret of Jesus"? It is not merely the joy and peace of self-renunciation that Jesus sets forth to His disciples. It is the inward qui- *Trust in a* etude and rest of self-surrender to a loving *sovereign* *Father.* Father who is also the Mighty God. And it is not from the sense of His resistless power, but from the consciousness of His love, of His Fatherhood, that peace comes. " Yea, Father, for so it was well-pleasing in Thy sight." [1] "Father, all things are possible unto Thee ; remove this cup from Me : howbeit not what I will, but what Thou wilt." [2] " Father, into Thy hands I commit My spirit." [3] This is the secret of Jesus. He does not teach bare sovereignty to which we must yield be- cause it is irresistible. He teaches sover- eignty of a certain kind, — the sovereignty of a Father, who is as much better, as He is more powerful, than all earthly parents or rulers, and who will never forsake His world, nor suffer His children to slip from His mighty hand.

III

But sovereignty of this kind necessarily im- plies distinctions in the manner of its exercise. It cannot possibly be conceived of in terms of

[1] St. Matt. xi. 26.   [2] St. Mark xiv. 36.   [3] St. Luke xxiii. 46.

The highest kind of sovereignty discriminates.

any single force or confined to any one mode of operation. It must be flexible and discriminating. It must include within itself as many forms of rule as there are forms of being under its dominion. What, for example, should we say of a king who had but one way of dealing with all his subjects, young and old, wise and ignorant, loyal and disloyal, and who treated his servants under precisely the same conditions as his horses and his chariots? Or what should we say of a father who attempted to regulate and rule his children without reference to their character, and who made no distinction between them and the furniture of his house? Yet this, in effect, is the theory of the divine sovereignty which has frequently been set forth by theologians as if it were the only one which did justice to the glory of God.

A lower kind of sovereignty mechanical.

"The will of God," according to this theory, "is the irresistible force. It is the source of all things, all persons, all events. From it they all proceed, under it they all act, by an invariable necessity. This will has already determined from all eternity everything that comes to pass. Every character in the world, like every rock and every plant, is just what God willed it to be. Everything that happens, happens because He willed it and precisely as He willed it. The life of mankind is far from being in any sense a voyage, an adventure, a probation. It is simply the process of printing a history which has already been written and set in type down to the last letter. The great press is in motion. Our souls are the blank pages. On one is printed a foreordained prayer. On another a foreordained blasphemy. Death is the folding knife. Judgment is the act of binding, in which the fair pages will be preserved and the foul pages rejected and burned. The sovereignty of God is exercised in seeing that the book goes through the press exactly as it was written, without the addition or subtraction of a single syllable of the foreordained text."

But surely, even if this theory were true and could be proved, it is not of a nature to give aid and comfort to those who are zealous for the glory of God. It does not really exalt and magnify the divine sovereignty, but narrows and degrades it. It does not call for the perfect wisdom and unlimited resources of a potent Ruler able to meet emergencies, to overcome oppositions, to guide and direct intelligent and free subjects like Himself, and to conduct a high enterprise, through all the difficulties that may arise, to a successful end. It calls for

The lower kind less glorious.

qualities of a lower kind and a strictly limited scope; the exact knowledge and the applied strength of a skilful machinist; not the broad intelligence, the swift genius, the inexhaustible patience, and the triumphant personal influence of a great Captain, a Master and Lord of men.

Which kind has God chosen?

It is conceivable, of course, that God might have chosen to create a universe in which His sovereignty should be exercised in this one unvarying line of foreordained necessity. Being supreme, He has both the right and the power to make such a sphere, or spheres, for the revelation of His attributes as may please Him. But it is not humanly conceivable that He should have made this particular choice which is ascribed to Him for His own glory. If He had chosen this kind of a universe, so far as we can see, it must have lowered and hidden His glory. It must have left Him with a field in which the highest qualities of personality could not possibly be exercised. It must have made all subsequent choice, and all approval or disapproval, and all truly moral government impossible. The existence of rewards and punishments, the sense of merit or demerit among the creatures of such a world, would be inexplicable. Nay more, it would be a cruel delusion, which, since it must come like everything else, according to this theory, from the will of the Maker, would reflect a dark shadow of discredit upon His moral character. To claim that this sense of responsibility, like all other parts of the system, may be a necessity, a legal fiction which is essential to the working of a scheme far above our comprehension and therefore above our judgment, makes it more awful, but not more admirable. If there is any validity whatever in our moral instincts, we need not hesitate to say, that from our present point of view, which is for us the only one attainable, this theory of the absolute and unconditional sovereignty of God, exercised by one law of necessity over all creatures, is so far from being for God's glory that it is apparently for His shame and dishonour.

As a matter of fact, it has been, and still is, the most fertile mother of doubts. "A universe in which all the power was on the side of the creator, and all the morality on the side of creation, would be one compared with which the universe of naturalism would shine out as a paradise indeed."[1] The idea of an irresponsible God ruling by an eternal and inflexible *fiat* over responsible men, is a moral nightmare,

The difficulties of absolutism.

[1] *Foundations of Belief*, p. 326.

under which humanity groans, and from which it struggles to awake, even though it should have to open its eyes upon the blank darkness of an unsearchable night. Between the unknowable God of agnosticism and the unlovable God of absolutism, there is indeed little to choose. But the choice, such as it is, lies on the side of agnosticism. It is unspeakably better to doubt God's personality, His supremacy, His very being, than it is to doubt His eternal goodness and His moral integrity.

Jesus delivers us from them.

But the teaching of Jesus is designed and fitted to deliver us, if we will accept it, from both of these doubts. He reveals a God who is not only Lord of all, but who exercises His sovereignty in discretion, in justice, and in love. He does not look upon all His creatures with the same eyes. He discriminates, He distinguishes, He has regard to their differences of nature and character. The human soul is of more value to Him than many sparrows.[1] How much is a man better than a sheep?[2] By so much as he is more like God, spiritual, free, responsible, immortal. These qualities, which God Himself has created, God Himself respects. Every word of Jesus takes it

[1] St. Matt. x. 31.   [2] St. Matt. xii. 12.

for granted that God is not an infinite Auto- *God is a fair master.*
crat, a hard master, reaping where He has not
sown, and gathering where He has not strewed,
but a fair and equitable Lord, who takes into
consideration all the conditions of His subjects
and renders unto all their dues. The forces of
nature obey His will inevitably, and for them
there is neither praise nor blame. The souls
of men are invited to love Him, and commanded to serve Him, but they are left free to
choose whether they will obey or disobey, and
upon their choice the approval and blessing of
God depend.

Who can question for a moment that this is *The divine*
the view of the divine sovereignty which un- *omnipotence self-limited*
derlies all the parables of Christ? The omnip- *in action.*
otence which He teaches is not sheer, absolute,
unconditioned. It is a self-restrained power.
It is able to limit itself, to act in such a way
and under such conditions as God chooses to
create. If He could not do this, He would not
be truly omnipotent. If there were but one
method in which He could manifest His will,
and that the method of necessity, He would be
forever shut out from personal relations, which
can only exist where there are different wills,
capable of agreement or disagreement, of co-
operation or conflict, of harmony or discord.

Jesus believed and taught that God has actually chosen to limit the autocratic exercises of His sovereignty by creating beings who have the power of yielding to His will or of resisting it.

The origin of evil not in God.

And from this resistance flow all the evil, all the sorrow, all the misery of the world. God does not ordain sin. God does not even permit sin, in the sense that He allows it to exist without opposition and condemnation on His part. It may be a necessary feature of a world of free choice and moral probation. Jesus seems to imply as much when He says " It must needs be that offences come." But He adds at once, " Woe unto that man by whom the offence cometh." [1] That man is not doing the will of God. He is a rebel, a traitor, an apostate. Sin is a perversion of the heart from its true purpose just as blindness is a perversion of the eye from its true function.[2] When the tares appear in the field, Christ does not leave us to suppose for a moment that they were planted by the same hand that sowed the good seed. He says, " An enemy hath done this." [3] Satan, who is the embodiment of evil and the leader of all who are opposed to God,

[1] St. Matt. xviii. 7.   [2] St. Luke xi. 34–36.
[3] St. Matt. xiii. 28.

is the great enemy, the adversary not only of souls, but also of the Divine will.

Turn for a moment to the narrative of the temptation of Christ.[1] He was led up by the Spirit into the wilderness to be tempted of the devil. But did the same Spirit lead the devil? Was Satan acting under the divine sovereignty in the same sense, in the same way, that Jesus was? Set aside, if you will, the question of the personality of the evil one. There was a suggestion of evil before the mind of Jesus. Did that suggestion come from the same source as the holy strength that resisted it, — the all-creating, all-controlling will of God? Can the same fountain send forth sweet and bitter waters? Why then should the one be called cursed and the other blessed? Such a view simply obliterates all moral distinctions. It completely undermines and ruins the significance of Christ's life as a free obedience to the will of God, and it utterly paralyzes His gospel as a divine call to men to enter freely into the same obedience.

Sin is the work of an enemy.

Jesus teaches very distinctly that there are two spheres in which the sovereignty of God is exercised, — in heaven and on earth.[2] These

Two spheres of God's sovereignty.

[1] St. Matt. iv. 1–11.
[2] Beyschlag, *New Testament Theology*, vol. i., pp. 84, 85.

two spheres are not conceived locally but spirit-
ually.   They are realms in which the power of
God is working under different conditions.   In
Triumphant   heaven the Divine will is unopposed, and there-
in heaven.   fore the empire of heaven is peace and holiness
and unbroken love.   On earth the Divine will
is opposed and resisted, and therefore earth is
a scene of conflict and sin and discord.   For
this reason the kingdom of heaven must *come*
to earth, it must win its way, it must strive
with the kingdom of darkness and overcome it.
God's sovereignty in heaven is triumphant.
Militant   God's sovereignty on earth is militant, in order
on earth.   that it may triumph, — and triumph not in universal destruction, but in the salvation of all
who will submit to it and embrace it and work
with it, — triumph not by bare force, as gravi-
tation triumphs over stones, but by holy love,
as fatherly wisdom and affection triumph over
the reluctance and rebellion of wayward children.

Divine   It must be admitted frankly that this view
omni-   of Divine sovereignty does not seem to be
science.   consistent with the theory of absolute divine
foreknowledge of all volitions and all events.
This has been urged as a fatal objection against
it.   But the objection cannot be pressed because

it lies in a region where our ignorance is so great that dogmatism is, to say the least, unbecoming. There may be some way of reconciling the self-limitation of God's omnipotence with the certainty of His foreknowledge, which is beyond the reach of our logic. But whether there be any such reconciliation or not, one thing is clear: we have not the right to make a logical statement of our ignorance of one divine attribute a reason for refusing to accept, frankly and sincerely, Christ's revelation of the mode in which another divine attribute is exercised.

God knows everything. But when we say that, we mean simply that He knows everything which can be the object of knowledge. He knows all things as they are. He does not know them as they are not. The very perfection of His knowledge consists in its exact correspondence with the nature of its object. If an event is certain, fixed, and foreordained, then God knows it as certain, fixed, and foreordained. If it is contingent upon the free, self-determining, preferential action of a human will, then God knows that it is contingent, for He Himself has foreordained that it should be so. *Foreknowledge corresponds with the facts.*

God waits to hear whether His children will call upon Him in their distress; and if they *God waits.*

call, He hears and helps them. If Jesus teaches anything, He teaches that prayer really influences the purpose and action of God.

The proba-tion of men.

God waits to see whether His husbandmen will return to Him the fruits of His vineyard; whether they will receive and honour the messengers whom He sends unto them; and if they are rejected, He sends other messengers; and last of all He sends His Son, saying, "It may be they will reverence him." [1] But when this last *maybe* does not come to pass, then judgment falls upon the wicked husbandmen, not because they have fulfilled the secret will of the King, but because they have rebelled against Him.

The Lord of Hosts.

This conception of God in His world, not as the mere spectator of the fulfilment of His own immutable decrees, but as the Lord of Hosts, presiding over the great scene of conflict between good and evil in the souls of men who can only attain to real holiness through real liberty, and warring mightily on the side of good in order that it may win the victory, infinitely exalts and glorifies Him. We see Him in the teaching of Jesus, as the High Captain of the armies of love, working salvation in the midst of the earth, pleading with men to accept His mercy, warning them

[1] St. Luke xx. 13.

to escape from His judgments, sustaining the good in their goodness, overthrowing the wicked in their wickedness, bringing light out of darkness and triumph out of defeat, amid all strifes and storms maintaining His kingdom of righteousness and peace and joy in the Holy Ghost. His sovereignty embraces human liberty as the ocean surrounds an island. His sovereignty upholds human liberty as the air upholds a flying bird. His sovereignty defends human liberty as the authority of a true king defends the liberty of his subjects, — nay, rather, as the authority of a father tenderly and patiently respects and protects the spiritual freedom of his children in order that they may learn to love and obey him gladly and of their own accord. For this is the end of God's sovereignty : that His kingdom may come ; that His will may be done on earth, — not as it is done in the circling of the stars or in the blossoming of flowers, — but as it is done in heaven, where created spirits freely strike the notes that blend in perfect harmony with the music of the Divine Spirit, where

Sovereignty embraces liberty.

> " Thousands at his bidding speed
> And post o'er land and ocean without rest;
> They also serve who only stand and wait."

IV

Does this create uncertainty?

But does not the acknowledgment that God has thus limited the operation of His sovereignty on earth by conditioning His actions upon the character and conduct of other beings than Himself, throw us back into confusion and uncertainty? Does it not make the course of the world insecure and the end of all things doubtful?

The reserve of power.

It would do so if it were not for the other truth which Jesus reveals with equal clearness, that God is in the world guiding, ruling, and directing it, and that He has kept the supremacy in His own hands. His presence is the talisman of creation. He is the master of the ship; His hand is on the helm; and whether the sailors obey or mutiny, He will guide the vessel to her appointed haven.

Evil transient, good eternal.

The power of evil is a finite, transient, self-destroying power. It disintegrates, it dies, it passes away with the enfeeblement and destruction of the soul that yields to it. But the power of goodness is eternal and incorruptible, because it is of God. Satan is the prince of this world, but his might is limited to the perverted and enslaved wills that submit to him. He is not the ruler of nature.

God is the master of winds and waves and
earth and stars. The great battalions are on
His side and under His control. If for one
instant the cause of Christ were in real danger, He could summon celestial hosts without
number to His assistance.[1] But because He
knew this, He knew also that His cause was
never in danger. He knew that His kingdom
was an everlasting kingdom. He knew that
He had already overcome the world.

How serene and splendid are the words with
which He reassures His disciples, again and
again ! *"Fear not! Care not! Be not anxious! O thou of little faith, wherefore didst thou
doubt? Have faith in God! Upon this rock
will I build my church and the gates of hell shall
not prevail against it! Fear not, little flock, for
it is your Father's good pleasure to give you the
kingdom!"* How glorious is the vision of that
kingdom which Jesus unfolds as He looks forward to the new birth of earth and heaven in
the perfect fulfilment of the purpose of God!
How absolute is the confidence with which He
rests upon God's power to work out all that
may be needed to bring about that blessed
consummation. The unwavering faith of Jesus
in the permanence and world-wide diffusion and

*God the
rock of our
trust.*

[1] St. Matt. xxvi. 53.

T

ultimate triumph of His kingdom of truth and holiness and love, is not the least — sometimes I think it is the greatest — evidence of His divinity and charm of His gospel.

The inspiration of heroism.

Communicated by His divine influence to the hearts of His disciples, this faith has been a force of incalculable potency and inspiration in the lives of men. The noblest deeds of heroism and self-sacrifice and liberation have been wrought in the strength of it. The greatest conquests over self and sin, the supreme victories of righteousness and love and peace in human hearts, have been won through this faith. *Deus vult* — God wills it! — is the war-cry that rouses the human will to its highest endeavour.

The secret of courage.

Here is a man struggling against evil, longing and striving to rise to high and holy life. And if he is alone in the struggle, what assurance has he, what promise or hope of success? He may fail, he may perish. But when the great truth flashes into his heart that God is with him in the fight, that God is "not willing that any should perish but that all should come to repentance,"[1] that God is the captain of his salvation and the leader of his soul, — then he is emancipated, then he triumphs, then he is joined to the Invincible. He cries

[1] 2 Pet. iii. 9.

with Paul, "If God is for us, who is against us?"[1]

Here is a saint called to endure sharp and heavy trials, to drink the bitter waters of affliction, to pass through the fires of pain, to go down into the dark valley of the shadow. Alone, it would be impossible; human patience could not endure it, human courage could not face it, human wisdom could not solve the mystery of goodness called to suffer. But with God, believing that He is sovereign, and that He is love,— how different it is! Now you shall see the wondrous spectacle of a frail, gentle, mortal soul, strengthened by simple submission to God's will, persecuted but not forsaken, cast down but not destroyed, trembling but victorious. Such a soul cries: "The will of God be done. It cannot be His will that I should lose my faith. It cannot be His will that I should deny Him. It cannot be His will that I should be lost, for He is good, He is my King, my Father, He will save me. It may be His will that I should suffer trial for the purifying of my faith, for a more perfect fellowship with Christ, for a better reward in heaven. Even so, Father, for so it seemeth good in Thy sight."

The strength of endurance.

[1] Rom. viii. 31.

"I welcome all Thy sovereign will,
    For all that will is love;
And when I know not what Thou dost,
    I wait the light above."

*God in
history.*

How radiant and magnificent is that truth
as it appears in the history of the Church.   The
people of God have often been persecuted and
oppressed, yet God has been on their side, and
no weapon that has been formed against them
has prospered.   Here is Philip of Spain send-
ing his great Armada to crush the Reformed
Church of England and destroy religious liberty in the cradle.   Like a huge flock of vul-
tures with outspread wings and fierce talons
and harsh innumerable cries of menace, that
most terrific company of war-ships that ever
darkened air and sea swoops towards its prey.
But the wrath of God meets it on the ocean,
and drives disorder through its serried ranks;
the swift little ships of England pierce it, and
break its wings, and riddle it with terror; its
onset is changed to flight, and as it flies, the angry
blasts of heaven and the wild waves of wrath
catch it again, and whirl it away, and scatter
on a hundred rocky shores and lonely beaches
the wrecks and fragments of the lost Armada.
How often has that wondrous history been
repeated!   How often has God proved His

sovereignty by preserving and rescuing and delivering His people from overwhelming perils! Even when it has seemed to be otherwise, even when the Church has appeared forsaken and helpless, when the billows of persecution have rolled fathom-deep above her head, when avalanches of falsehood have buried the truth out of sight, it has only been for a time, and the end has been the victory of the defeated. The blood of the martyrs has been the seed of the Church. The boastful shouts of error have been the advertisement of the silent truth. Error has had kings and generals, philosophers and orators, empires and armies; truth has had God. Error has had swords and spears, ships and cannons, fortresses and dungeons, racks and fires; truth has had God. God and one make a majority. Unless the Church doubts, she cannot fear. Unless the Church denies, she cannot despair. In the darkest days, when the confusion seems greatest, the conflict most unequal, she can look out on the great battle-field and cry

Truth and God.

"History's pages but record
One death-grapple in the darkness 'twixt old systems and
    the Word;
Truth forever on the scaffold, Wrong forever on the
    throne, —

Yet that scaffold sways the future, and behind the dim
    unknown
Standeth God within the shadow, keeping watch above
    His own." [1]

*The victory
is sure.*

But is it for the Church alone, is it not for
the whole world that this truth of God's sovereignty shines? To our eyes the conflict of
life and death, of good and evil, seems to be
undecided, and we think it may be perpetual.
The dust blinds us; the uproar bewilders us;
as far as our sight can pierce we see nothing
but the rolling strife, — sin always in arms
against holiness, the created will always resisting and defying the creator. But Christ sees that
the conflict is decided, though it is still in progress. Christ sees that the victory is won,
though it is not yet manifest. On the hill of
the cross the captain of salvation met the captain of sin and conquered him. Calvary is
victory. Through death Christ hath overcome
him that had the power of death, that is the
devil.[2] Satan has received his mortal wound;
and if he still fights more fiercely, it is because
he knoweth that he hath but a short time.[3] The
day is coming when he must perish; the day is
coming when sin and strife shall be no more;

*The final
consumma-
tion.*

[1] James Russell Lowell, *The Present Crisis.*
[2] Heb. ii. 14.   [3] Rev. xii. 12.

the day is coming when Christ shall put all enemies under His feet[1] and shout above the grave of death, "O thou enemy, destructions are come to a perpetual end"; the day is coming when the great ship of the world, guided by the hand of the Son of God, shall float out of the clouds and storms, out of the shadows and conflicts, into the perfect light of love, and God shall be all in all. The tide that bears the world to that glorious end is the sovereignty of God.

> O mighty river, strong, eternal Will,
> In which the streams of human good and ill
> Are onward swept, conflicting, to the sea, —
> The world is safe because it floats in Thee.

[1] 1 Cor. xv. 25–28.

VIII

SERVICE

"Thyself and thy belongings
Are not thine own so proper as to waste
Thyself upon thy virtues, they on thee.
Heaven doth with us as we with torches do,
Not light them for themselves; for if our virtues
Did not go forth of us, 't were all alike
As if we had them not.   Spirits are not finely touched
But to fine issues; nor Nature never lends
The smallest scruple of her excellence,
But, like a thrifty goddess, she determines
Herself the glory of a creditor —
Both thanks and use."

— *Measure for Measure.*

VIII

SERVICE

THAT strange and searching genius, Nathaniel Hawthorne, in one of his spiritual phantasies has imagined a new Adam and Eve coming to the earth after a Day of Doom has swept away the whole of mankind, leaving their works and abodes and inventions, — all that bears witness to the present condition of humanity, — untouched and silently eloquent. The representatives of a new race enter with wonder and dismay the forsaken heritage of the old. They pass through the streets of a depopulated city. The sharp contrast between the splendour of one habitation and the squalor of another, fills them with distressed astonishment. They are painfully amazed at the unmistakable signs of inequality in the conditions of men. They are troubled and overwhelmed by the evidence of the great and miserable fact that one portion of earth's lost inhabitants was rich and comfortable and full of ease, while the multitude

This uneven world.

was poor and weary and heavy-laden with toil.[1]

The sense of distress at life's inequality. This feeling of sorrowful perplexity over the unevenness and apparent injustice of human life, which the prose poet puts into the heart of his new Adam and Eve, is really but a reflection from the tender and pitiful depths of his own. Who is there that has not sometimes felt it rising within his own breast, — this profound sentiment of inward trouble and grief, this feeling of spiritual discord and wondering repugnance at the sight of a world in which the good things of life are so unequally distributed, in which at the very outset of existence, before the factor of personal merit or demerit, the element of work and wages, enters into the problem at all, so much is given to one man and so little to another man that they seem to be forever separated and set at enmity with each other by the unfairness with which they are treated?

The sympathy of the age. This sentiment has been strangely deepened and intensified in the nineteenth century by innumerable causes, until it has become one of the most marked characteristics of the present age. Never before have men felt the sorrows

[1] Hawthorne's Works, Riverside Edition, 1884; *Mosses from an Old Manse*, p. 297.

and hardships of their fellow-men so widely, so keenly, so constantly as to-day. In one sense this is the honour and glory of our age. It is an evidence of quickened moral sensibility, a revival or renewal of the noblest capacities of our human nature.

But in another sense it is the greatest peril of our age. For it has been seized by the spirit of scepticism and transformed into an ally of annihilating doubt. It has been used as an argument against the possibility of discovering a moral order in such a "hungry, ill-conditioned world" as this. Man's inhumanity to man has been employed to prove God's indifference or injustice to man. The feeling of sorrow and perplexity has been aggravated by wild and whirling words into a passion of resentment against the present conditions of life. Rash and sweeping schemes for their total destruction have been proclaimed as a new gospel. Christianity has been first claimed as a supporter of these schemes, and then denounced and repudiated as the chief obstacle to their success. The cry goes up that the whole world is out of joint. "Everything is wrong and crooked and unfair : the race of man has been deceived and maltreated and oppressed by the creation of such an order of

A noble sentiment driven to madness.

life as the present. If God created it, so much
the worse for God. But it is almost certain
that He did not create it, almost certain that
there is no God. The world of inequality is
man's mistake. There is but one thing to do,
and that is to break it all up, at once and
utterly, and begin anew. Create a new world
if possible. If not, then let the old wreck sink
and be blotted out, for it is worse, infinitely
worse, than the blank desolation of an unconscious chaos."

*What shall
we do?*
This cry of anger and despair rings to-
day in the ears of all earnest and thoughtful
men and women. The element of sincerity,
of truth, of justice, that thrills unmistakably
through its strange, fierce music, stirs our
hearts to the core. We are filled with perturbation and distress and deep anxiety to
know the right and to do it, to understand the
meaning of this exceeding great and bitter cry,
and the duty to which it calls us. Is it indeed
the utterance of true equity and wisdom? Is
it the voice of a new Adam, appearing after so
many ages of delusion, with open eyes to condemn the old world, and with ruthless hand to
break it in pieces? Must we welcome him and
hearken to him and believe in him, as the true
judge and regenerator and leader of mankind?

The very form of the question points the *Christ's* way to the only Master who can answer it. *answer and example.* Hawthorne's picture of the second Adam was a poetic dream. But the Apostle Paul uses the same figure to reveal a historic truth. " The first man Adam became a living soul. The last Adam became a life-giving spirit. Howbeit that is not first which is spiritual, but that which is natural; then that which is spiritual. The first man is of the earth, earthy; the second man is of heaven." [1] The new Adam has already come upon the earth, eighteen centuries ago. He was called Jesus. With pure and perfect heart He entered into the world, not desolate and depopulate, but thronged with the myriads of toiling, suffering men. With clear eyes He looked upon their different conditions, their manifold inequalities, their outward and inward joys and sorrows. With steadfast heart He set Himself to the divine task of beginning a new humanity and inaugurating the kingdom of heaven on earth.

He did not strive nor cry, neither was His *His calm-* voice heard in the streets.[2] He did not protest *ness and sanity.* against the moral government of the universe, because one man was rich and another poor, one strong and another weak, one happy and

[1] 1 Cor. xv. 45–47. [2] St. Matt. xii. 19.

another wretched, one good and another evil. He did not say that God must be unjust because He has given, in things spiritual as well as in things temporal, much to one and little to another.   He did not teach His followers that the only way to help the world was to rebel against this order, and refuse to submit to it, and denounce it, and fight against it. He did not even proclaim a social and political revolution.   He was the most peaceful, orderly, obedient, loyal citizen of all that subject land of Palestine ; rendering unto Cæsar the things that were Cæsar's, discharging every duty of His lowly lot with cheerful fidelity, and labouring patiently for His daily bread.

He knows the secret.

He was not blind, nor dull of heart to feel the troubles of life.   The problem of inequality lay wide open before Him.   But it did not agitate nor distract Him.   He neither raved nor despaired.   He was serene and sane.

"He saw life clearly and He saw it whole."

He looked through the problem to its true solution.   He knew the secret which justifies the ways of God to man.   He knew the secret by which an eternal harmony is to be brought into the apparent discords of life.   He knew the secret by which men living in an unequal world, and accepting its inequality as the condition of their present existence, can still become partakers of a perfect, peaceful equity, and citizens of an invisible, imperishable city of God. That secret was none other than the highest, holiest doctrine of Jesus, the divine truth of election to service.

I

Before we set our hearts to take in the meaning and the fulness of this truth, let us try to get them in tune for it by listening to some of the other teachings of Jesus which are meant to quiet and steady us in the contemplation of the unevenness of human existence. *Christ's gospel for the present world.*

And first of all He reminds us that our real happiness in this world does not depend upon our outward condition, but upon our inward state. " The life is more than meat and the body than raiment."[1] "A man's life consisteth not in the abundance of the things which he possesseth."[2] The land of wealth is not the empire of peace. Joy is not bounded on the north by poverty, on the east by obscurity, on the west by simplicity, and on the south by servitude. It runs far over these borders on

[1] St. Matt. vi. 25.   [2] St. Luke xii. 15.

U

every side.   The lowliest, plainest, narrowest
life may be the sweetest.   Most of the disciples
of Jesus were peasants, but they were as happy,
as contented, even in this world, as if they had
been princes.   There was more gladness and
singleness of heart in that frugal breakfast of
broiled fish and bread beside the boats on the
shore of the sea of Tiberias,[1] than in the
splendid feast in the house of Simon the Phari-
see.   Life has its compensations and its com-
forts for all estates.   Work means health.
Obscurity means freedom.   The best pleasures
are those that are most widely diffused.

The secret of   I do not mean to say that Jesus overlooked
happiness.   the bitter hardships of toil under bad masters,
under false and cruel and oppressive laws.   I
do not mean to say that He would not have
been full of pity and indignation at the sight
of the crushed and crippled state of great multitudes of human beings in our modern cities.
But I am sure that He teaches us to believe
that the real source of human misery is not in
poverty, but in a bad heart; that envy is not a
virtue, but a vice ; that life is a great gift to all
who will receive it cheerfully and contentedly,
even in a world where its material things are
unevenly distributed ; and that the true beati-

[1] St. John xxi. 1-13.

tudes are not monopolies reserved for the few, but blessings within the reach of all, and gloriously independent of all outward contrasts in the lives of men. Indeed it seems as if He would go even beyond this, and remind us that some of these blessings could not be ours except in a world of contrast and temporal inequality. Of the eight beatitudes which Jesus Himself pronounced, four at least, — the blessing of the mourners, and of the meek, and of the merciful, and of the peace-makers, — imply the existence of differences and degrees among men; and one — the blessing of those who are persecuted for righteousness' sake — is only possible in a world where evil is sometimes actually more powerful and prosperous than good.

I have not been able to find a single word of Christ that looks forward to a time in which there shall be no more inequalities on earth, no more rich and poor, no more masters and servants, no more wise men, and no more babes. But there are many words of His that pierce with mild and gracious light through all these outward distinctions to reveal the truth that this kind of inequality is superficial and illusory, that the babes rejoice in beholding those mysteries which are hidden from the wise and pru-

The compensations of life.

dent, that servants are often nobler and more free than their masters, that the poor may have treasures laid up in heaven which are beyond all earthly reckoning, and that this is the true wealth which brings contentment and peace.

Peace on earth.

It is a great mistake to suppose that Jesus preached a gospel which was melancholy and depressing for those who received it in this world. It is a great mistake to suppose that He taught men that they must resign themselves to earthly misery and make the journey of life as a weary and mournful pilgrimage. He came to cheer and brighten the hearts of all who would accept His guidance and tread the path of virtue with courage and fidelity and hope. He came to give us rest in the midst of toil, and that refreshment which only comes from weariness in a good cause. He came to tell us not to despair of happiness, but to remember that the only way to reach it on earth is to seek first usefulness, first the kingdom of God, and then the other things shall be added. He that loseth his life for Christ's sake shall not lose it but find it,[1]—find it in deep inward contentment,

"And vital feelings of delight,"

[1] St. Matt. x. 39.

which make up the true and incomparable joy of living.

Jesus does not differ from other masters in that He teaches us to scorn earthly felicity. The divine difference is that He teaches us how to attain earthly felicity, under all circumstances, in prosperity and in adversity, in sickness and in health, in solitude and in society, by taking His yoke upon us, and doing the will of God, and so finding rest unto our souls. That is the debt which every child of God owes not only to God, but also to his own soul, — to find the real joy of living. *The secret of felicity.*

> "Joy is a duty," — so with golden lore
> The Hebrew rabbis taught in days of yore.
> And happy human hearts heard in their speech
> Almost the highest wisdom man can reach.
>
> But one bright peak still rises far above,
> And there the Master stands whose name is Love,
> Saying to those whom heavy tasks employ
> "Life is divine when duty is a joy."

Joy is a duty.

The second point in the teaching of Jesus which is meant to rectify our views of the unevenness of the world, is His doctrine of a future life, — not a different life, but the same life moving on under new conditions and to new issues. This world is not all. There is another world, a better age, a more perfect state of being, in which *The world that is to come.*

the sorrows and losses of those who now suffer
unjustly will be compensated, and in which —
let us not hesitate to say it as calmly and as
firmly as Jesus said it — those who have unjustly and selfishly enjoyed their good things
in this world will suffer in their turn. It is
the fashion nowadays to sneer at such teaching
as this; to call it "other-worldliness"; to
declare that it has no real power to strengthen
or uplift the hearts of men. Jesus did not
think so. Jesus made much of it. Jesus
pressed home upon the hearts of men the con-
solations and warnings of immortality. He
showed the miserable failure of the man who
filled his barns and lost his empty soul.[1] He
bade His disciples, when they suffered and were
persecuted for righteousness' sake, "rejoice and
be exceeding glad, for great is your reward
in heaven."[2]

*The errors
of time call
for the
balance of
eternity.*

Let us not impoverish our gospel by flinging
away, in our fancied superiority, this precious
truth. It is impossible to justify the present
fragmentary existence of man if we look at it
and speak of it as the whole of his life. Earth
has mysteries which naught but heaven can
explain. Earth has sorrows which naught but
heaven can heal. Yes, and earth has evils,

[1] St. Luke xii. 16–21.   [2] St. Matt. v. 12.

black and secret offences of man against man, false and foul treasons against the love of God, crimes which take a base advantage of His patience and long-suffering and hide themselves like poisonous serpents in the shelter of the very laws which He has made for the good of the world, sins all entangled with the present structure of society and beyond the reach of human law, undiscoverable iniquities, unpardonable and unpunishable cruelties,—which naught but hell can disclose and consume. The errors of time call for the balance of eternity. Patient labour, patient endurance, patient resignation in this present life shall be greatly rewarded in the life to come. Now is the day of toil and trial; but the pay-day will surely dawn. Much of the best that is done in this world receives no earthly wages. Those to whom it is done,—the poor, the maimed, the lame, the blind,—"they cannot recompense thee; but thou shalt be recompensed at the resurrection of the just." [1]

Thus Jesus teaches; and He shows us that the present order of inequality, so far from being an obstacle to this result, is the very means by which it is to be accomplished. The discipline of this uneven life is the education

This unequal life our education for the future.

[1] St. Luke xiv. 14.

by which alone we can be prepared for the heavenly life. Jesus does not present Himself as a rectifier of life's unequal conditions of outward fortune. He distinctly refuses this office. "Man, who made me a judge or a divider over you?"[1] Jesus does not preach an equality which is synonymous with life on a dead level. He does not preach equality at all. He preaches fraternity. And fraternity implies differences, — older and younger, stronger and weaker, higher and lower. The elder brother is the heir; all that the father has is his; but his sin lies in holding fast to his inheritance selfishly, in shutting out his younger brother, in forgetting and denying that he is a brother at all.[2] The distinctions of life are not meant to obscure, but to reveal and to beautify its best virtues. Out of dependence spring the sweet blossoms of gratitude and loyalty. Out of mastership flow the refreshing streams of forbearance and justice and mercy. The apostle tells us that the love of money is a root of all kinds of evil.[3] But Christ shows us the deeper truth that the right use of money is a means of all kinds of good. "It is more blessed to give

Fraternity better than equality.

---

[1] St. Luke xii. 14.   [2] St. Luke xv. 25–32.
[3] 1 Tim. vi. 10.

than to receive."[1] Every gift of Providence
to us is an opportunity and therefore a responsibility, and the blessing does not come
with the gift until we recognize the responsibility, and use the opportunity. The mammon
of unrighteousness can only be destroyed by
a process of transformation which transmutes
it into the pure gold of the celestial treasury.[2]
The name of that process is charity. And the
translation of that name is wise and holy
love.

Let us try to think distinctly. It is said *Christianity*
nowadays that Christianity means communism, *and Com-*
munism.
and that it is the duty of all Christians to
give away everything that they possess. It
is strange that Christ never proclaimed this
duty except to one man, and that man was not
a Christian.[3] Of course it must be admitted
at once that this would be the duty of all
Christians if it could be shown that it would
be for the real good of their fellow-men. But
this never has been shown. On the contrary,
communism has always turned out badly. It
was tried in Jerusalem, in a limited way, when
the early Christians sold all that they had and
made a common purse; but it led, in less

[1] Acts xx. 35.   [2] St. Luke xvi. 19.
[3] St. Mark x. 21.

than ten years, to confusion and strife, and
sank the Jerusalem church into a condition
of pauperism and dependence upon the other
churches, which had avoided the well-meant
but dangerous experiment. It was tried in
France, under atheistic auspices, and its fruit
was wide-spread misery and injustice. It was
tried to some degree in England, under a system of poor laws which were based upon the
idea that every man had a right to eat whether
he would work or not, and it resulted in such
disorder and demoralization that it had to be
discarded as a menace to society.

*Love thy
neighbour
as wisely
and well as
thyself.*

There is nothing in the teachings of Christ
which would make us blind to these plain
lessons of history. On the contrary, He desires and commands us to discover and do that
which will really bless and help our fellow-
men. "Thou shalt love thy neighbour as thyself," [1] — the same kind of love, the same inward regard for the higher ends and aims of
life, which is the saving grace of the individual soul, is to be the saving grace of society. And what kind of love is that? It
is a wise and holy love, a love which puts
character first and comfort second, a love which
seeks to purify and bless and uplift the whole

[1] St. Matt. xxii. 39.

man. Such a love may be shown by withholding as truly as by bestowing. False charity pampers self and pauperizes others. True charity educates self by helping others. The so-called Christian who never gives is a false Christian. The Christian who gives carelessly, blindly, indiscriminately, however generously, is a very imperfect Christian. The Christian who gives thoughtfully, seriously, fraternally, bending his best powers to the accomplishment of a real benefaction of his fellow-men, bestowing himself with his gift, is in the true and only way of the following of Jesus.

Preach this truth. Preach it home to the hearts of men, without fear or favour for rich or poor. *Every privilege is a call to service.* Preach it home to your own heart so close that it shall save you from the minister's besetting sins of spiritual selfishness and cant. Tell the Lady Bountiful that she is not called to discard her ladyhood, but to give herself with all her refinements, with all her accomplishments, with all that has been given to her of sweetness and light, to the ennobling service of humanity. Tell the Merchant-Prince that he is not called to abandon his place of influence and power, but to fill it in a princely spirit, to be a true friend and father to all who are dependent upon him, to make his prosper-

ity a fountain of blessing to his fellow-men, to
be a faithful steward of Almighty God. And
then let us tell ourselves, as members of the
so-called "educated classes," to whom God has
given even greater gifts than those of rank and
riches, — privileges of knowledge, opportunities
of culture, free access to the stored-up wisdom
of the ages, — let us tell ourselves with unflinching fidelity that God will hold us to a
strict account for all these things. If our salt
loses its savour it shall be trodden under foot
of men. If our culture separates us from humanity we shall be cast into the outer darkness.
Our light must shine or be shamefully extin-
guished. Every faculty and every gift we
possess must be honestly and entirely consecrated to the service of man, in Christ's name
and for Christ's sake. This is the gospel for
the present age, and for every age. This is
Social re- the way in which the kingdom of heaven is to
generation. be established on earth. This is the way in
which the inequality of this mortal life is to
be transfigured and irradiated with a divine
equity. "What we look for, work for, pray
for, as believers, is a nation where class shall
be bound to class by the fullest participation
in the treasure of the one life; where the mem-

bers of each group of workers shall find in their work the development of their character and the consecration of their powers : where the highest ambition of men shall be to be leaders of their own class, so using their special powers without waste and following the common traditions to noble issues : where each citizen shall know, and be strengthened by the knowledge, that he labours not for himself only, nor for his family, nor for his country, but for GOD."[1]

II

Thus far the teaching of Christ leads us with clear serenity in our understanding of the differences among men in the distribution of the goods of this present world. But the deeper problem still remains untouched. There is an apparent inequality in the bestowal of spiritual blessings. In the life of the soul also, it seems that much is given to one and little to another. Some men are born very close to the kingdom of heaven and powerfully drawn by unseen hands to enter its happy precincts. Other men are born far away from the gates of light, and it looks to us as if all the influences of their life were hindrances rather than helps to holiness.

Inequality in the spiritual world.

[1] B. F. Westcott, Bishop of Durham, *The Incarnation and Common Life* (London, Macmillan, 1893), p. 82.

There is an undeniable contrast in the religious world which can only be interpreted as a divine foreordination, — that is to say, an act by which some men are set before others, given the precedence, offered an earlier and apparently an easier opportunity of spiritual life. If God is sovereign, this act, by which the means of grace are unevenly dispensed, must be the result of a divine choice.

The doctrine of election.

The formal recognition of this choice is the doctrine of election. It is an inevitable doctrine. It is founded upon facts which admit of no denial. And it brings every thoughtful and earnest soul face to face with the question of questions, upon the answer to which the nature and reality of religion depend.

The searching question.

Is God arbitrary, is God partial, is God unjust? Does He bless some of His children and leave the rest under an irremediable curse without a single reason which can be exhibited to human faith and justified in perfect love? In the last and highest realm of life, the realm of the spirit, does He make it more blessed to receive than to give, and exercise His sovereignty in favouritism, and establish heaven as a kingdom of infinite and eternal and inexplicable inequality?

False answers.

It is an idle thing to answer this question by an appeal to God's absolute right to dispose of all His creatures as He will. For the very *An arbi-trary God.* essence of true religion is the faith that He is such a God that He wills to dispose of all His creatures wisely and fairly and in perfect love. And the very essence of a true revelation, as the message which calls religion into being, is that it makes God's wisdom and fairness and love manifest, and so helps us to understand and adore and trust Him, not only for ourselves but for the whole world.

It is an idle thing to answer this question by *An irrespon-sible God.* saying that God is under no obligation to be good to everybody, and therefore that He may be good to whomsoever He pleases. The idea of an irresponsible God is a moral mockery. Poisonous doubt exhales from it as malaria from a swamp. To teach that all men are God's debtors, and that therefore it is right for Him to remit the debt of one man, and to exact the penalty from another to the last farthing, is to teach what is logically true and morally false. Our hearts recoil from such a doctrine. If God has made us, and made us spiritual paupers, utterly incapable of anything good, we are not His debtors. Jesus teaches us that God asks of us only to give as freely as we have received.[1] He demands only that which He

[1] St. Matt. x. 8.

Himself has made us able to pay. And He forgives like the good master in the parable, with a free pardon which needs but the confession of helplessness and poverty to call it forth.[1]

A God whose glory is not goodness.

It is an idle thing to answer this question by an appeal to ignorance, and to say that God elects some men to be saved and leaves the rest of mankind to be lost simply for His own unsearchable and inexplicable glory! For God's glory, as revealed by religion, is identical with His goodness. Faith, true and joyful and uplifting faith, answers only to a gospel which makes that identity more clear and luminous, and shows that the divine election in the realm of grace is perfectly consistent with that wide and deep love wherewith God so loved the whole world that He sent His only begotten Son that whosoever believeth in Him should not perish but have everlasting life.

Election perverted in human theology.

Now it is because men have forgotten this that they have found no answer, or a false and misleading answer, to the problem of inequality in the spiritual world. It is because they have torn the doctrine of election from its roots in the divine love, and petrified it with unholy logic, that it has lost its beauty, its perfume,

[1] St. Matt. xviii. 27.

its power of fruitfulness to everlasting life.
We must go back from the dead skeleton as it
is preserved in the museum of theology to the
living plant as it blossoms in the field of the
Bible. We must go back of Jonathan Edwards,
and back of John Calvin, and back of Augustine,
to St. Paul, and see how, under his hand, all
the mysterious facts of election as they are
unfolded in human history, break into flower
at last in the splendid faith that "God hath
shut up all unto disobedience that He might
have mercy upon all."[1] We must go still
farther back, to Christ, and learn from Him
that election is simply the way in which God
uses His chosen ones to bless the world, —
the divine process by which the good seed is
sown and scattered far and wide and the
heavenly harvest multiplied a thousand-fold.
"I elected you," He says to His disciples and
to us, "I elected you, and appointed you, that
ye should go and bear fruit, and that your fruit
should abide."[2]

Christ's doctrine of election is a living, *Christ's doc-*
fragrant, fruitful doctrine. It is the most *trine of*
election to
beautiful thing in Christianity. It is the very *service.*
core and substance of the gospel, translated

[1] Romans xi. 32.
[2] St. John xv. 16.

x

from the heart of God into the life of man. It is the divine law of service in spiritual things. It is the supreme truth in the revelation of an all-glorious love ; the truth that God chooses men not to be saved alone, but to be saved by saving others, and that the greatest in the kingdom of heaven is he who is most truly the servant of all.

Christ as the elect servant.

Is not this true of Christ Himself ? He is the great example of what it means to be elect. He is the beloved Son in whom the Father is well pleased. And He says " Behold, I am in the midst of you as he that serveth."[1] Service was the joy and crown of His life. Service was the refreshment and the strength of His soul, the angel's food, the "meat to eat" of which His disciples did not know.[2]

The disciple must be as his Lord.

Was not this the lesson that He was always teaching them by practice and by precept, that they must be like Him if they would belong to Him, that they must share His service if they would share His election! "I have appeared unto thee for this purpose," He said to Saul, "to make thee a servant (ὑπηρέτην, *a rower in the ship*), and a witness both of those things which thou hast seen and of the things

[1] St. Luke xxii. 27.
[2] St. John iv. 32.

in the which I will appear unto thee."[1] The
vision of Christ is the call to service. And if
Paul had not been obedient to the heavenly
vision could Saul have made his calling and
election sure? But he answered it with a noble
faith. "It pleased God to reveal His son in
me *in order that I might preach him among
the nations.*"[2] Henceforward, wherever he
might be, among his friends in Cilicia, in the
dungeon at Philippi, on the doomed vessel
drifting across the storm-tossed Adriatic, in
the loneliness of his Roman prison, this was
the one object of his life, to be a faithful servant of Christ, and therefore, as Christ was, a
faithful servant of mankind.[3]

How can we interpret Christ's parables, with- *Parables of privilege and service.*
out this truth? The parables of the Pounds
and the Talents are both pictures of election
to service. They both exhibit the sovereignty
of God in distributing His gifts; they both
turn upon the idea of man's accountability for
receiving and using them; and they both declare
that the reward will be proportioned to fidelity in serving. The nature and meaning of
this is explained by Christ in His great description of the judgment, which immediately follows the parable of the Talents in St. Matthew's

[1] Acts xxvi. 16.   [2] Gal. i. 16.   [3] 2 Cor. iv. 5.

Gospel.[1] Many of those who have known **Him**
will be rejected at last because they have not
served their fellow-men.   Many of those who
have not known Him will be accepted because
they have ministered lovingly, though igno-
rantly, to the wants and sorrows of the world.
Service, the
key-note of
the king-
dom.
Service is the key-note of the heavenly kingdom, and he who will not strike that note shall
have no part in the music.   The King in the
parable of the Wedding Feast[2] chose and called
his servants, not to sit down at ease in the
palace, but to go out into the highways and
bid every one that they met, to come to the
marriage.   And if one of those servants had
refused or betrayed his mission, if he had neglected his Master's business, and sat down on
the steps of the palace or walked pleasantly in
the garden until the supper was ready, do you
suppose that he would have found a place or a
welcome at the feast?   His soul would have
stood naked and ashamed without the wedding-
garment of love.   For this is the nature of
God's kingdom, that a selfish religion absolutely unfits a man from entering or enjoying
it.   Its gate is so strangely strait that a man
cannot pass through it if he desires and tries

[1] St. Matt. xxv. 31–46.
[2] St. Matt. xxii. 1–13.

to come alone; but if he will bring others with
him, it is wide enough and to spare.

> Who seeks for heaven alone to save his soul,
> May keep the path, but will not reach the goal;
> While he who walks in love may wander far,
> Yet God will bring him where the blessed are.

How wonderfully all this comes out in the *The prayer of interces-* great intercessory prayer of Christ at the last *sion.* supper.[1] That prayer is the last and highest
utterance of the love wherewith Christ, having
loved His own which were in the world, loved
them unto the end.   He prays for His chosen
ones : " I pray for them : I pray not for the
world but for those whom Thou hast given Me."
" Holy Father, keep them in Thy name which
Thou hast given Me, that they may be one even
as We are.   For their sakes I consecrate Myself,
that they themselves also may be consecrated
in truth.   Neither for these only do I pray, but
for them also that believe on Me through their
word ; that they may all be one, even as Thou,
Father, art in Me, and I in Thee, that they also
may be in Us ; that the world may believe that
Thou didst send Me."   How the prayer rises,
like some celestial music, through all the interwoven notes of different fellowships, the fellowship of the Father with the Son, the fellowship

[1] St. John xvii.

of the Master with the disciples, the fellowship
of the disciples with each other, until at last it
strikes the grand chord of universal love.   Not
for the world Christ prays, but for the disciples
in the world, in order that they may pray for
the world, and serve the world, and draw the
world to faith in Him.   And so, in truth, while
He prays thus for His disciples, He does pray
for the whole world.   Circle beyond circle, orb
beyond orb, like waves upon water, like light
from the sun, the prayer, the faith, the conse-
crating power spread from that upper room
until they embrace all mankind in the sweep of
the divine intercession.   The special, personal,
elective love of Christ for His own is not
exclusive ; it is magnificently and illimitably
inclusive.   He loved His disciples into loving
their fellow-men.   He lifted them into union
with God ; but He did not lift them out of
union with the world ; and every tie that
bound them to humanity, every friendship,
every fellowship, every link of human intercourse, was to be a channel for the grace of
God that bringeth salvation, that it might
appear to all men.[1]

Christ's ideal.

This is Christ's ideal : a radiating gospel :
a kingdom of overflowing, conquering love ; a

[1] Titus ii. 11.

church that is elected to be a means of blessing to the human race. This ideal is the very nerve of Christian missions, at home and abroad, the effort to preach the gospel to every creature, not merely because the world needs to receive it, but because the Church will be rejected and lost unless she gives it. 'Tis not so much a question for us whether any of our fellow-men can be saved without Christianity. The question is whether we can be saved if we are willing to keep our Christianity to ourselves. And the answer is, No! The only religion that can really do anything for me, is the religion that makes me want to do something for you. The missionary enterprise is not the Church's afterthought. It is Christ's forethought. It is not secondary and optional. It is primary and vital. Christ has put it into the very heart of His gospel. We cannot really see Him, or know Him, or love Him, unless we see and know and love His ideal for us, the ideal which is embodied in the law of election to service.

For this reason the spirit of missions has always been the saving and purifying power of the Christian brotherhood. Whenever and wherever this ideal has shined clear and strong, *Missions essential to Christianity.*

it has revealed the figure of the Christ more
simply and more brightly to His disciples, and
guided their feet more closely in the way of
peace and joy and love.

*Missions
emancipated
the early
church.*

In the first century it was the spirit of foreign missions that saved the Church from the
bondage of Jewish formalism. Paul and his
companions could not live without telling the
world that Christ Jesus came to seek and save
the lost — lost nations as well as lost souls.
The heat of that desire burned up the fetters
of bigotry like ropes of straw. The gospel
could not be preached to all men as a form of
Judaism. But the gospel must be preached to
all men. Therefore it could not be a form of
Judaism. The argument was irresistible. It
was the missionary spirit that made the Eman-
cipation Proclamation of Christianity.

*Missions
keep the
gospel pure.*

In the dark ages the heart of religion was
kept beating by the missionary zeal and efforts
of such men as St. Patrick, and St. Augustine,
and Columba and Aiden, and Boniface, and
Anskar, who brought the gospel to our own
fierce ancestors in the northern parts of Europe
and wild islands of the sea. In the middle
ages it was the men who founded the great
missionary orders, St. Francis and St. Dominic,
who did most to revive the faith and purify

the life of the Church. And when the Reformation had lost its first high impulse, and sunken into the slough of dogmatism; when the Protestant churches had become entangled in political rivalries and theological controversies, while the hosts of philosophic infidelity and practical godlessness were sweeping in apparent triumph over Europe and America, it was the spirit of foreign missions that sounded the *reveillé* to the Christian world, and lit the signal fire of a new era — an era of simpler creed, more militant hope, and broader love — an era of the Christianity of Christ. The desire of preaching the gospel to every creature has drawn the Church back from her bewilderments and sophistications closer to the simplicity that is in Christ, and so closer to that divine ideal of Christian unity in which all believers shall be one in Him. You cannot preach a complicated gospel, an abstract gospel, to every creature. You cannot preach a gospel that is cast in an inflexible mould of thought, like Calvinism, or Arminianism, or Lutheranism, to every creature. It will not fit. But *the* gospel, the only gospel which is divine, must be preached to every creature. Therefore, these moulds and forms cannot be an essential part of it. And so we work our way back out of the tangle of human speculations toward that pure, clear, living message which Paul carried over from Asia to Europe, the good news that God is in Christ, reconciling the world to Himself.

*One mes-
sage and
many ways
of preach-
ing it.*
This is the gospel for an age of doubt, and for all ages wherein men sin and suffer, question and despair, thirst after righteousness and long for heaven. There are a thousand ways of preaching it, with lips and lives, in words and deeds ; and all of them are good, provided only the preacher sets his whole manhood earnestly and loyally to his great task of bringing home the truth as it is in Jesus to the needs of his brother-men. The forms of Christian preach-ing are manifold. The spirit is one and the same. New illustrations and arguments and applications must be found for every age and every race. But the truth to be illuminated and applied is as changeless as Jesus Christ Himself, in whose words it is uttered and in whose life it is incarnate, once and forever. The types of pulpit eloquence are as different as the characters and languages of men. But all of them are vain and worthless as sound-ing brass and tinkling cymbals, unless they speak directly and personally and joyfully of that divine love which is revealed in

Christ in order that all who will believe in it may be saved from doubt and sin and self-ishness in the everlasting kingdom of the loving God.

This is the gospel which began to shine through the shadows of this earth at Bethlehem, where the Son of God became the child of Mary, and was manifested in perfect splendour on Calvary, where the Good Shepherd laid down His life for the sheep. For eighteen centuries this simple, personal, consistent gospel has been the leading light of the best desires and hopes and efforts of humanity. It is the one bright star that shines, serene and steady, through the confusion of our perplexed, struggling, doubting age. He who sees that star, sees God. He who follows that star, shall never perish. It has dawned upon my heart so clearly and so convincingly that the one thing I have cared and tried to do in these lectures is to make it plain that this is the essence of Christianity, the only gospel that is worth preaching in all ways to all men, that Jesus Christ is God who loves us in order that we may learn to love one another. But if I have failed to make this view of religion clear, if an imperfect utterance has beclouded and obscured the message, at least let this last word be plain, at least let nothing hide

The only gospel.

from your soul or from mine, this supreme, saving truth of election to service.

The last word.

The vision of God in Christ is the greatest gift in the world. It binds those who receive it to the highest and most consecrated life. To behold that vision is to be one of God's elect. But the result of that election depends upon the giving of ourselves to serve the world for Jesus' sake. *Noblesse oblige.*

Believers in Christ, the servants of God's love to the whole world.

Let us not miss the meaning of Christianity as it comes to us and claims us. We are chosen, we are called, not to die and be saved, but to live and save others. The promise of Christ is a task and a reward. For us there is a place in the army of God, a mansion in the heaven of peace, a crown in the hall of victory. But whether we shall fill that place and dwell in that mansion and wear that crown, depends upon our willingness to deny ourselves and take up our cross and follow Jesus. Whatever our birthright and descent, whatever our name and profession, whatever our knowledge of Christian doctrine and our performance of Christian worship may be, — when the great host is gathered in the City of God, with tattered flags and banners glorious in their bloodstained folds, with armour dinted and swords worn in the conflict, with wounds which

tell of courage and patient endurance and
deathless loyalty, — when the celestial knight-
hood is assembled at the Round Table of the
King, our name will be unspoken, our crown
will hang above an empty chair, and our place
will be given to another, unless we accept now,
with sincere hearts, the only gospel which can
deliver us from the inertia of doubt and the
selfishness of sin. We must enter into life by
giving ourselves to the personal Christ who un-
veils the love of the Father in a Human Life,
and calls us with Divine Authority to submit
our Liberty to God's Sovereignty in blessed
and immortal Service to our fellow-men **for**
Christ's sake.

INDEX

319

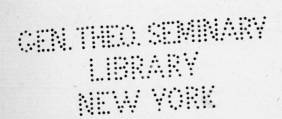